THE GREAT BETRAYAL

The Elite's War on Middle America

by

Louis T. March

and

Brent Nelson

THE GREAT BETRAYAL

ISBN: 1-887898-00-X

Order from:

Representative Government Press
P. O. Box 97668, Raleigh, NC 27624

Contents

Introduction

The hall was heavy with stale, sticky, stifling air. Fifty-six of the richest men in the land were cooped up in it for hours, chafing from discomfort far greater than that of the summer heat. They risked their lives in that room, doing something for which, if they were caught, they would be killed—no question. But they did it anyway, openly and publicly signing their probable death warrant: the Declaration of Independence. This was treason, pure and simple—punishable by death in the eyes of the British Crown. The July 4, 1776 Declaration put fifty-six lives, families and fortunes squarely in harm's way. Why did they do it; what for? Perhaps we can take comfort in the fact that they didn't do it for free; they did it for freedom.

What kind of people would do such a thing? They were elite—the elite—the richest men around—with the most land, biggest homes, finest horses, and nicest clothes. Why would they, of all people, with so much to lose, risk certain death? Would the wealthiest people in America today—the current elite—lay their very lives, much less their money on the line for freedom? The obvious answer to that question is a most revealing sign of the times.

Elite of character and courage, the fifty-six who risked the gallows unleashed a fury that changed the world. Five years and thousands of lives later on October 16, 1781 a military band played "The World Turned Upside Down." The occasion was the surrender of Lord Cornwallis, the

British commander, to General George Washington. And the world *was* turned upside down. A Revolution was won which had originally sprung into action amid cries of "No taxation without representation!" The victory of the ragtag Continental Army over the forces of the mighty British Empire shocked the world—and marked the downfall of imperial rule in our land. We the People were no longer colonies ruled from afar, but were becoming a new self-governing republic. Representative Government was soon born in the Constitution of the United States of America — a great nation that was to become the guiding light of the modern world.

That elite—gentlemen of distinction like George Washington, Samuel Adams, Patrick Henry, Benjamin Franklin, Thomas Jefferson, and Richard Henry Lee—risked it all. They were not career politicians (there was no such thing) and took it seriously to heart that they were sworn and entrusted to serve—not master—the people. They had no notion of enriching themselves at cost to others. They possessed a natural nobility and were so bound to the soil, folk and faith of their land that when they spoke there was no question that We the People—one people—were speaking. They labored for the common good: the well being of all.

Now, more than two hundred years later, another Revolution has occurred, a gradual yet complete betrayal of the first American Revolution: **The Great Betrayal**. Imperial rule has returned. Taxation without representation is back. We have the finest Congress money can buy, with law and social policy handed down by unelected Federal Judges and bureaucrats. The American dream is being taken from us; and our great Constitution poses little threat to the current form of government.

We no longer have Representative Government in America. Yes, we continue to hold elections, solemn oaths of office are uttered on solemn occasions, and glorious pronouncements are broadcast from the highest quarters all about democracy, family values, civil rights and justice. But the Emperor has no clothes. That great government of the people, by the people, and for the people has died the death of a thousand cuts. We have simply been betrayed— big time.

The Great Betrayal did not come upon us overnight—it has been long in the making. The 1930s Depression brought about the welfare state, and the World War which ended it spawned the military industrial complex. Both, for better or for worse, were predicated upon big government. This signaled the rise of a big government coalition in American politics: the military-industrial-welfare state. It is a corporate welfare state where power lies not with the people but with multinational corporations and the government. If there is any doubt, look how often the establishment transcends conservative-liberal-Republican-Democrat divisions to take care of what is really important to them: (NAFTA, Peso bailout, etc.) Yes, they are in it together. Though the Depression had ended and the World War was won, this big government status quo thrived through the Cold War and beyond, fueled by massive government deficits and financed with the hard-earned tax dollars of a trusting American middle class. The self-serving agenda and unmitigated greed of the corporate welfare state elite has thoroughly corrupted our system of government.

Majority rule is gone. If there is any doubt, consider the following:

The majority were overwhelmingly opposed to forced busing for racial balance—we have it.

The majority were opposed to the Panama Canal Treaties—they passed.

The majority are opposed to current levels of taxation—have been for years.

The majority are opposed to the massive federal deficits—makes no difference.

The majority are opposed to the thirty-year crime wave—whole sections of our major cities are not safe. Criminals walk.

The majority are opposed to massive illegal immigration—so what? It continues year after year.

The majority opposed the U.S. bailout of the Mexican peso—too bad.

The majority are opposed to so-called affirmative action—it's still around.

The majority don't understand why their sons should be sent to fight and die for Somalia, Haiti, Bosnia and other parts unknown—tough.

The majority favor a Balanced Budget Amendment to the Constitution—still waiting.

The majority favor term limits on Congress—don't have it.

The majority want a better standard of living—real wages have been falling for over two decades.

Every nation is led by an elite; but prodigious Middle America provided the soldiers, the labor, the energy and general wherewithal for the United States to become a leading force in the world. Yet since the Depression and World War II, the American elite has become international in character, profiting greatly from economic "globalism." They have abandoned stewardship of the domestic body politic. The result has been the disempowerment of the middle class, a trend with dangerous long-term implications. This dispossession of Middle America can be seen in much of current domestic and foreign policy. *The Great Betrayal* seeks to examine several areas where the Betrayal is obvious: trade, foreign aid, family policy, welfare, firearms rights, deficits and more.

The filthy rich elite at the helm today is quite different from those noble souls who risked it all to lead us in 1776. Today's elite does not think of America as We the People, a proud nation, but solely as an economic unit, a labor force, a gigantic piece of real estate where money can be made. They have more in common with their financial peers around the globe than with the average American. And they couldn't care less. Their economic unit world view respects no nation, culture or people except as markets, labor and consumers. They believe in open borders, undefended markets, big government and grand schemes. If they worship anything, it is the almighty dollar. To them money is an end in itself, our national well being an expendable means in pursuit thereof. They believe that government and capital exist not to serve the people, but that the people are to serve big government and big business. They have been penny wise and pound foolish with our money. Their policies have spawned a huge welfare underclass and depressed the American standard of living for a generation. This is the demise of Representative Government in our country—and it is a very dangerous state of affairs.

The United States is now a debtor nation, essentially bankrupt, ruled from an imperial capital, with little or no control of our borders, streets or domestic economy. Extra-constitutional government—imperial rule from Washington and Wall Street—arrogantly presides as the foreign acquisition of our assets, depletion of our resources, and the confiscation, through every conceivable means, of the fruits of our labors proceeds apace.

We are a colony anew; newly colonized over a period of time to serve a globalist agenda of unmitigated greed. The interests of our own hard-working citizens have been subordinated to the grand designs of a transnational elite. The brunt of internal imperialism's burden falls squarely upon the American middle class, who are called upon—rather commanded—to finance GATT, NAFTA, foreign aid, bureaucracy, welfare and every other scheme imaginable. This corrupt process is killing the American Dream, and for the first time in the memory of any living American, the up and coming generation does not anticipate the level of prosperity known to their parents.

America is a great country; Americans are a great people. We deserve the kind of government bequeathed to us by the Founding Fathers—of the people, by the people, for the people. *The Great Betrayal* examines the alarming dispossession of Middle America. In reviewing this sad state of affairs, a few ideas are offered as to what the average citizen can do to take back our country. As the old saying goes, without a solution you may be part of the problem.

Abandoned by the powers that be in favor of big government and easy money, the whole of Middle America should collectively seize the reins and lead a crusade to reclaim national prosperity and resurrect Representative Government in our land.

Chapter One

Downsizing the American Dream

A short generation ago the greatest country on the face of the earth realized an impossible dream: America put a man on the moon. But not only was the American Dream evident in outer space—right here at home one American worker with a high school diploma could support a family. Anytime in American history before the 1970s, the average worker—farmer, stevedore or salesman, it didn't matter—could support his family better and better with each ensuing generation. Nowadays most people find supporting a family on one income is just about as difficult as going to the moon. What happened?

Could it be that a very powerful force—someone or something somewhere unseen—has changed the rules of the game? Has our social contract, the American Dream—which generations of Americans have come to believe in and depend on—been canceled? Educated young people look longer and harder for jobs. Veteran workers find no security in seniority—or in their pension funds. Multinational corporations increasingly treat their employees like equipment—with minimum maintenance, lower operating costs, built in obsolescence and cheap off-shore replacements. There was prosperity aplenty when this started, so why not? Nowadays when pink slips appear, retraining and counseling programs are the solution. Those fortunate enough to keep their jobs receive lower, adjusted-for-inflation pay than the previous generation. This has been the trend since 1973—there is something dreadfully, dreadfully wrong.

Even after the Depression and World War II, the American Dream was back on track with a vengeance. A 1950s high school graduate signed on at the factory, worked hard, and in a few years had enough to marry, buy a house and raise two or more children while his wife could stay at home. It now seems amazing that a family could ever do all that on one income. Nowadays Middle Americans need at least two full-time incomes to buy an average house and raise a smaller family. The typical married couple are workers almost to the exclusion of being husbands, wives or parents. As leisure time dries up, all the politically correct talk about "quality time" makes no difference.

The national tragedy is that our households are no longer safe—physically or financially—as they were a generation ago. Are we better off than ever before just because we own more VCRs, computers and CD players? Many of these consumer goods are now made in Japan, or profits from their sale and manufacture go to Japan or elsewhere. Is that good for the U.S. economy? Does the dollar value of these gadgets offset the crunch in affordable housing or the increased struggle to support fewer children? What about the decrease in leisure time and the resultant impoverishment of family life? Better off than ever? Don't bet on it.

Look at the government's own data. The U.S. Department of Commerce compiles "average weekly earnings" statistics for production or nonsupervisory personnel—80 percent of all employees. Manufacturing workers were just 17 percent of the workforce in 1992; so most people with declining wages and salaries were in the so-called services economy. This includes a huge number of white collar workers. So much for the notion that the big move from blue collar to white collar work has been a middle class milestone. Allowing for inflation, "average weekly earnings" have continued to decline since 1973. Economist Wallace Peterson calls this a "silent depression." Seventy-five percent of Americans have experienced an average earnings decline of 19 percent since 1973. The decline continues with no end in sight. Most people are not better off than ever.

Some are hit worse than others. By 1991 average manufacturing earnings had fallen to 1965 levels; construction workers' earnings to 1961 levels; and retail trades employee earnings had regressed to below 1950's levels. (These figures allow for inflation and are found in the *Council of Economic Advisers' Economic Report of the President*, U.S. Gov't. Printing Office, 1992.)

This tragic decline in living standards has been covered up by statistics. Yes, per capita household incomes have risen. But those higher numbers are from two full-time workers; and from more time on the job for each (overtime, overwork, etc.). The average American worker put in 95 hours more in 1987 than he did in 1979—well over two work weeks! With dual incomes, more working time and a smaller family to support, household per capita income is up—just like buying power, correct? Here again the statistics will fool you—apparent buying power is certainly up—along with personal debt and credit. But sooner or later debts must be paid. Carrying enormous debt is not real prosperity. And sooner or later it will catch up with us—just look at the U.S. Government.

The 1980s were a most interesting time. In that decade the wealthiest one percent of our fellow citizens enjoyed phenomenal income growth (mostly unearned income). Congressional Budget Office figures say that from 1977 to 1989 almost 60 percent of personal income increase went to the top one percent. From 1983 to 1989, the national share of net assets held by the one percent club leaped from 31 to 37 percent. Between 1984 and 1988, the net worth of the

400 richest Americans doubled. Great PR about good times at the top overshadowed the really big story of the 1980s— the sharp drop in average earnings for working people and those dependent on fixed incomes.

Inflation hit retirees hard. The next generation of fixed income people face an even more bleak future. With employer participation way off, they increasingly fend for themselves to fund their own retirement plans. 401(k) plans were almost unknown fifteen years ago; by 1994 they outnumbered conventional plans by numbers of 40 million to 36.5 million. Many 401(k) enrollees end up needing that money for medical bills, mortgages and automobiles—their own retirement money!

By the 1980s America had the widest spread between rich and poor of any western country. The middle class here had become a smaller percentage of the population than in Norway, Switzerland, Sweden, Germany and Holland. Our top one percent prospered as never before; the upper 20 percent or so held their own; almost 80 percent of Americans lost ground. A Middle American economic holocaust is in progress.

The President's Council of Economic Advisors calls "a widening gap between rich and poor a threat to the social fabric." They blamed the growing disparity on "technology, the decline of unions, a lagging minimum wage and, to a lesser degree, immigration." They denied that competition with foreign workers was a factor in the decline of American wages, *but admitted that as a future possibility.*

Another reason for the top one percent windfall is a most bizarre practice of American corporations: rewarding top management irrespective of performance. When profits decline and workers are laid off, CEOs prosper. During 1991 General Motors lost $4.5 billion; IBM, $2.8 billion; Ford, $2.3 billion; and Westinghouse, $1.1 billion; while chief executives of these corporations earned, respectively,

$1.6 million, $4.9 million, $1.6 million and $3.3 million. While some of these corporations now operate in the black, job losses have been staggering. Is downsizing what turning around a company is all about? Eliminating jobs by the thousands? There has been no comparable downsizing of CEO compensation. America has long been notorious for the absurd compensation packages ladled out to corporate chief executives. In 1990 the average American CEO earned more than 100 times that of the average American worker. Japanese and German CEOs earned, respectively, 20 and 35 times average worker earnings but presided over corporations frequently more productive than their American counterparts. This does not speak well for America—or at least for some of those in power in America.

Capital speculation, including "insider trading," yields the largest take by far, outpacing greedy CEOs by multiples. Renegade traders such as Ivan Boesky and Michael Milken filched tens of billions from the American economy. And there are thousands of aspiring Boeskys out there just an attorney's fee within the letter of the law. Arbitrage, speculation, derivatives gambling and other money manipulation—as opposed to genuine productivity, entrepreneurship and wealth creation—are circular processes that do not go on forever.

If all this isn't bad enough, working Americans pay a much larger share of the total tax burden than a generation ago. State sales taxes and Social Security taxes, both averaging around 2 percent in 1950, by 1991 had respectively soared to 7 percent and 7.65 percent. Take home pay is further chiseled away by all kinds of taxes. In 1948 the typical middle income family of four paid two percent of its income in income taxes—now that same family pays 24 percent of its income in income taxes alone! By 1990 both direct and indirect taxes at all levels were taking at least 37 cents out of every dollar earned. The average American family pays more in all taxes than it does for food, clothing and shelter combined! The current tax burden is a living nightmare—confiscation—a hate crime against Middle America.

Where does all this tax money go? A staggering amount goes to benefit the top one percent—our friendly elite! This includes covering "bad" loans and international banking commitments gone sour. The Panama Canal Treaties, third-world foreign aid and the multi-billion Mexican Peso bailout are examples. The gargantuan sums allocated to pay off the Savings and Loan scandal will probably cost the American taxpayer three hundred billion dollars (i.e., $300,000,000,000)! Another huge chunk of change (14 percent) goes to pay interest on the federal debt. At the state and local level, tax dollars pony up for tax-free municipal bonds (tax free for those who buy them, more taxes for many who have never seen a bond in their lives).

Much of our tax money not benefiting the wealthy goes for the elite's effort to subsidize, manage and control the growing criminal underclass and its unmitigated hatred and contempt for an America lashed to the yoke of its support. This is a pathological absurdity—a subsidy of hate. It is a state-run protection racket, harming the very people it is supposedly intended to help. There is no telling as to its total cost to society. Appeasement is expensive, and no amount of hate taxes on the middle class will ever make it work.

Job security crumbles right along with take-home pay. President Clinton, leading a political party which once upon a time had some legitimate claim as friend of the American worker, says we must accept the fact of changing careers—careers, not jobs—several times in our working lives. Clinton's message is of a new dark age of employment insecurity, a brave new world where the old concept of wage slave acquires reality anew. He effectively says there is nothing that government can do about it. Easy for Mr. Clinton to say. Career politicians rarely have to change careers!

Economic growth no longer means prosperity for most. Middle America is told that this is all part of economic expansion. Whose economy? There has been no expansion in household stability, community and security—yet a lot of money is being made. The "hidden hand" of the global "free market" does not have "America First" on its agenda. A cruel, vicious, America-neutral brand of laissez faire is trumpeted by the titular head of the Democratic party! But don't look to the Republicans for solace. Much of the GOP establishment interprets "The world doesn't owe anyone a living" to mean that the U.S. Government should do nothing to defend the American standard of living. While a growing number of rank and file in both parties actively support Middle American workers, their party leadership marched in lockstep to promote NAFTA, GATT and the gold-plated Mexican "Peso bailout." Bi-partisanship is dangerous!

Those lucky enough to find new work after layoffs usually come back for less. Sixty percent of jobs created during the first half of 1993 were part-time. This large-scale increase in transient and temporary workers is a sad signal of a wholesale slide into working poverty.

This Silent Depression features a flourishing elite, a hanging on top twenty per cent or so, and a floundering everyone else—while financial markets soar! In 1993 more people were laid off than had lost their jobs during the previous two years. This was almost two years after the 1991 recession was pronounced dead! Corporations launched into even more downsizing and "restructuring." IBM eliminated 80,000 employees; Sears, 50,000; Boeing, 28,000; Proctor & Gamble, 13,000. These were just a few among dozens of Fortune 500 companies with enhanced profitability from shedding excess employees. Remaining workers are told to work longer and harder for less. The May 4, 1995 *Wall Street Journal* headline summed it up: "Thanks, Goodbye: Layoffs Boost Profits but Also Increase Anxiety."

Downsizing makes for a lean and mean corporate world. IBM retrenched from 407,000 employees in 1986 to 215,000 by late 1994. Sears cut a total of 137,000 jobs by that time, down from 500,000 souls in 1990. Other corporate parings in 1994 alone were: Digital, 20,000; GTE, 17,000; Nynex, 16,800; Delta Air Lines, 15,000; AT&T, 15,000; Pacific Bell, 10,000; Scott Paper, 8,300; Boeing, 7,000; Fleet Financial, 5,500. Cutting jobs is a major way to boost the bottom line. There was a time when business did not see it that way.

Downsizing swept entire industries like a prairie fire. In 1993 the largest 100 American electronics firms eliminated a total of 480,000 jobs. John Stern of the American Electronics Association explained it in *Time* Magazine: "The American life-style is supported by manufacturing jobs. They are the entry point into the middle class for women and minorities and anyone else climbing the ladder who doesn't have the contacts or education to become a software engineer. These people can't lead a middle-class life in the service jobs that are left over."

While downsizing can help the bottom line, it doesn't always do the trick. *The Economist*'s comment on an American Management Association study: "fewer than half of the firms that have shrunk in the past five years subsequently raised their profits . . . Moreover, only a third of downsizers reported higher productivity." *The Economist* suggested that "battered employee morale" interfered with realizing the full benefits of downsizing. An AT&T executive has confessed: "In the past we said to employees: 'Do as you're told and you have a job for life.' Then we betrayed them. Trust levels were devastated."

Highly educated workers are not exempt. Job security is a thing of the past for scientists and engineers. During 1993 from 500 to 1,000 people were applying for each mid-level executive opening available. "When people talk about economic recovery," said Scott Scanlon, publisher of *Executive Search Review*, "people tend to think that means more jobs. There's not going to be a recovery in jobs."

Retraining programs are no replacement for a real job. And don't count on real jobs to materialize. Even the Department of Labor admitted that only 1 in 5 workers losing manufacturing jobs to foreign trade found new ones with at least 80 percent of the pay.

However, new jobs abound in the private security industry. Wonder why? By 1990 there were 1.5 million private security workers. Twice as much was spent on that industry than on public police forces. Practically every American city now has new wall-enclosed upscale housing. Can't blame them if they can afford the protection. Wealthy enclaves so defended have long been characteristic of the Third World.

Some so-called experts tell us this massive downsizing is just "the end of a 40-year postwar economic boom;" that normal workplace conditions were really not normal; it was just a temporary "postwar boom" situation. Fortune 500 (half the GDP) downsizing is predicted to continue until the year 2000 costing millions of jobs. This "postwar boom" propaganda is designed to explain away why an American worker cannot support his family in today's economy.

What postwar boom? Once vanquished Germany and Japan now enjoy an economic health surpassing that of the United States. German workers earn more than their American counterparts with uncomparable social services. (Much of America's so-called social services are underclass subsidies not readily available to the middle class).

Japanese worker incomes are almost as high as those of their American counterparts, and lack of job security is not an issue.

Since German and Japanese industry were rebuilt from the ruins, they did not enjoy America's postwar headstart. While massive U.S. aid fueled their reconstruction, allocation of human resources made a big difference as well. Japan graduates many more engineers than MBAs, the exact reverse of America's situation. And neither country mass produces attorneys as in the U.S. There is also a perception that German and Japanese industrialists are not as enamored with the notion of simply using money just to make money. Sony Corporation CEO Akio Morita put it this way: "Americans make money by playing 'money games,' namely mergers and acquisitions, by simply moving money back and forth . . . instead of creating and producing goods with some actual value." Mr. Morita may have a point.

Corporate downsizing and increased "temporizing" of employment are all part of global economic "expansion." The traditional American worker will eventually be replaced by powerless, degraded Third World labor if this agenda continues unchecked. Why else does the deluge of legal and illegal immigration continue? This is not some secret conspiracy. Representatives of the corporate welfare state—the big government/big business elite—are most forthright about their designs for a global economy of "levelized" earnings and lowered living standards throughout the Western Hemisphere and beyond. It is candidly discussed in scholarly journals not widely publicized in the popular media. The 1990 *Journal of International Affairs*, "U.S. Immigration Policy Toward Mexico in a Global Economy," explains that "the transformation of the occupational and income structure in the United States—itself in good part a result of the globalization of production—has created an expanding supply of low-wage jobs. The decline of manufacturing and the growth of services have contributed to make more jobs temporary and part-time, reduced advancement opportunities within firms, and weakened various types of job protection. The resulting casualization of the labor market facilitates the absorption of immigrants, including undocumented immigrants."

Middle America's gradual impoverishment at the hands of a greedy elite masquerades under many labels. Globalism, Free Trade and The Third Wave are among them. But it is wrong to think that any elite conspires to lower American living standards. They are simply out to make money, utilizing the levers of power at their disposal. They couldn't care less about the overall state of affairs apart from their money. They are busy. Falling living standards are just an incidental by-product of their business. The common people can fend for themselves and keep out of mischief with the jobs and entertainment provided. Middle American protests against new world order globalism are not a problem—so far.

The world view of today's elite is far from that of the noble elite who so courageously risked everything in 1776 and paved the way for unparalleled prosperity in our land. Today's greed-driven world view is a sad sign of the times; it is a callous "money-might makes right" attitude long prevalent in Third World economies.

This economic unit world view is spawning a new feudalism. But this kind of feudalism has nothing in common with the old aristocratic tradition of *noblesse oblige* wherein "noble birth imposes the obligation of high-minded principles and noble actions." In the feudalism of old Europe, the loyalty of the landless was returned with reciprocal loyalty and protection by the landlords.

There is nothing at all noble about today's American elite—only money commands their loyalty. God and

Country better get in line. No longer American in spirit, they are America-neutral, utterly cosmopolitan, totally self-serving, and ready to scour the ends of the earth for profit while their countrymen suffer increasing economic hardship. Preaching equality for all, this elite sets the rules of the game for Middle America but lives by different standards. The hypocrisy is obvious. Selling out America benefits their interests, buys off a threatening underclass, and makes money for them. That is Betrayal, pure and simple.

The leadership of both parties are part of the problem. Democrats propagandize that underclass poverty is the fault of Republicans, racism and Middle American complacency. Republicans max out on free-market Horatio Alger type rhetoric while intervening to taking care of the big boys. Is there more poverty or less? Where have the tax cuts been all these years? What about NAFTA? Yes, both parties wholeheartedly subscribe to the dogma of global "free trade." Nothing is free—so perhaps we should take a closer look at so called "free trade."

Chapter Two

"Free Trade"

There is no such thing as "free trade." The very phrase is a bald-faced politically correct deception designed to evoke notions of "freedom." It is a bogus concept. All trade and trade agreements have rules, so are by definition not "free" as corporate spin doctors would have us believe. If one party in a chess game selfishly changes their rules, the other side loses until they respond accordingly. When China, Japan and France make their own trading rules, what is the U.S. to do? Can we count on the World Trade Organization to look out for American interests? Or do we stick up for ourselves?

The "free" market is not God. We should defend our markets as we should defend our borders. American markets and American borders are important to American workers—but they are an inconvenience to today's transnational elite, which makes no distinction between foreign and domestic peoples, cultures or commodities. There is nothing at all "free" about a trade policy which would eventually consign millions of American workers to the bondage of perpetual poverty.

Free trade's antithesis, Protectionism, is what economists call autarky—defined as "a policy of national self-sufficiency and nonreliance on imports or economic aid." Thus Protectionism—an economic National Defense policy—stands for national economic independence. Free trade stands for international economic interdependence, where the well-being of producers and consumers in one country is highly dependent on producers and consumers in another. This is not good policy for our country—at all.

Free trade is freedom only for multinational corporations, freedom for them to operate unencumbered across national boundaries. It also frees them from any concern for the well-being of American workers. Freedom is usually won at great cost; the cost of free trade is the American standard of living—expensive indeed!

The 1776 Declaration of Independence was a resounding rejection of Britain's policy of colonial mercantilism which effectively outlawed manufacturing in the colonies. But the Declaration of Independence wasn't the only important development that year to affect world trade. Adam Smith's *The Wealth of Nations* was also published, which if applied today would be a declaration of free trade dependence. Smith knew that international trade was different from trade within a nation. He understood ways in which low-wage labor could possibly compete with higher-priced labor in a domestic market, but did not believe this could occur on an international scale. In Smith's day industrialists would not be willing to make the investment necessary to move their factories to other countries. It wouldn't make sense economically, and would conflict with loyalty to crown and country. Modern transportation and the close proximity of low-wage nations have invalidated Smith's argument in this century.

Most early American leaders (except Jefferson and Madison) did not accept Smith's economics, which benefited Britain first and foremost. They had no fear of factories leaving the country, fearing instead that American factories would never come into existence. President John Adams realized that free trade was bad for America. He wrote: "The British merchants and manufacturers, soon after the peace, disgorged upon us all their stores of merchandise and manufactures, not only without profit, but at certain loss for a time, with the express purpose of annihilating all our manufacturers." As a result of British action, even Jefferson and Madison came around to agree with Adams. Nowadays such disgorging of goods is known as dumping and is how the Japanese have gained control of major American consumer goods markets.

Benjamin Franklin, Alexander Hamilton and Henry Clay all fought for an "American System" of national political economy designed to jump start American manufacturing with protective tariffs. Clay stressed that free trade depended on "perpetual peace" and "perfect reciprocity," two conditions which can never be. The American System—the opposite of free trade—led our country to unprecedented prosperity and industrial development. Abraham Lincoln strongly defended it. By the end of the War Between the States, the United States was the second greatest industrial power in the world. Years later Theodore Roosevelt declared, "Thank God I'm not a Free Trader."

Perhaps the definitive debunking of free trade ideology was by German economist Friedrich List in his 1837 *The Natural System of Political Economy*. Among other things List pointed out that a society's economic wealth and well-being are determined not by what it can buy and consume, but by what the society can make. A national industrial base is much more important than any consumer market. America must be a strong producer first—consumer paradise second.

Of the forty U.S. presidents prior to George Bush, only Ronald Reagan and Grover Cleveland endorsed free trade. The Republican Party has traditionally favored protective tariffs. The free trade takeover of the GOP during the Reagan years reversed a 150-year bipartisan policy. Yet the seeds of this reversal were actually planted as Cold War strategy in the Truman administration. Alfred Eckes, former International Trade Commission chairman, tells the story in "Trading American Interests" (*Foreign Affairs*, Fall, 1992).

According to Eckes, from 1947 to 1972 average U.S. tariffs fell from approximately 32 percent to "a negligible 8.5 percent." This Cold War-driven policy bought the U.S. votes in the United Nations. It aided the economic recovery of Britain and other western allies, and sought to anchor the economies of former enemies Germany, Italy and Japan to that of the U.S. Another goal was to prevent technology transfer to the Soviet bloc and stave off economic calamity in the Third World. The latter, of course, has been a colossal failure. Since 1945 hundreds of thousands of American jobs have been sacrificed to create prosperity and employment elsewhere in the world.

While this policy may have helped U.S. foreign policy goals, its post-Cold War effect has been a growing deindustrialization of America. Yet the insanity continues. The U.S. buys China's cooperation at the U.N. with Most Favored Nation trade status. China has a virtually unlimited cheap labor pool waiting to be tapped by multinational corporations. And their prison camp labor rates are even cheaper! Cold War trade concessions to Japan are also coming back to haunt us. Japan is an economic powerhouse because of U.S. postwar largesse and their unyielding Protectionist national trade policy. Because of these policies, our uninterrupted 1893 to 1970 trade surpluses turned into trade deficits for 19 of the next 21 years. And it isn't getting any better.

As Communist regimes collapsed, our domestic economy weakened as well. According to Eckes, "implementation of the final Kennedy Round tariff cuts in 1972 coincides with the beginning of a twenty-year decline in domestic earnings and manufacturing jobs. Again, average American wages in 1991 were 20 percent below 1972 levels. Meanwhile, the textile and apparel industries lost over 600,000 jobs, while steel and automobiles sacrificed another 500,000 positions."

In *The Myth of Free Trade*, Professor Ravi Batra says that for the last eighteen years "for over three fourths of the nation, the living standard has declined by 19 percent, with no end in sight." This is not because of lesser productivity. "Ford Motors today," according to Batra, "produces roughly the same number of cars and trucks as in 1975 with only about half the number of employees. This means that worker productivity there has practically doubled in eighteen years, yet Ford workers have lower real earnings (adjusted for inflation) than they did in 1975."

The Cold War partial sellout of American workers was justified as a bloodless sacrifice against Soviet expansionism. We were told it was better to fight an economic Cold War than a hot thermonuclear war, a premise subject to challenge by veterans of the Vietnam "Cold War."

Whatever good Reagan/Bush free trade initiatives did in the Cold War, they are no longer valid. We simply can't go on trading away America's well-being for foreign policy triumphs. When President Bush attempted to mobilize international support to drive the Iraqis from Kuwait, Germany and Japan contributed almost nothing to the effort. Other Western allies denied the U.S. use of support facilities. New World Order economic cooperation did not extend to the battlefield.

The "perpetual peace" and "perfect reciprocity" necessary for free trade can never exist. As for "perfect peace," the U.S. is exposed to the disruptive effects of limited wars more than ever before. In 1840 it didn't matter if trade was cut off from a large part of the Middle East, source of today's fossil fuels, or from South Africa with its essential metals. What about "perfect reciprocity?" Disparities in world economic development today are the greatest in history. In 1840 all nations, with the exception of Britain, were essentially agrarian. Wage levels could not be strikingly different between national economies because wage-based economies largely did not exist.

What reciprocity can there be with Mexico? Even without protective tariffs, Mexican workers cannot become large scale consumers of expensive American products. With average wages at one-seventh that of American labor, *perpetual poverty* is a fair characterization of their existence. This doesn't bother the NAFTA/GATT cheerleaders one bit. It is the virtually unlimited cheap labor, the very impossibility of reciprocity, that attracts them.

Claims of reciprocity with Mexico are a sham. In 1992, $40.6 billion in U.S. "exports" went to Mexico—looks great on paper. But only 19 percent of these "exports," $7.7 billion worth, were of consumer goods. Of the remainder, $17.4 billion, 43 percent, were of parts for assembly in U.S.-owned plants for resale north of the border. And another $15.5 billion, 38 percent, were of capital goods, such as machinery and tools. So more than eighty percent of the U.S. "exports" to Mexico were not true exports at all but rather supplies and equipment mostly destined for use in U.S.-owned factories in Mexico. Yet deceptions like that helped NAFTA pass Congress.

Professor Harley Shaiken cites a big reason corporate America wants more Mexican trade: Ford workers in Hermosillo earn from one to six dollars an hour while Ford workers in Detroit earn forty dollars an hour including benefits. The low Mexican wages do not mean lower quality manufacturing. Ford Escorts coming out of the Hermosillo plant ranked fifth in quality out of forty-six Ford assembly plants in North America. In quality, they even surpassed the products of five Japanese-owned plants in North America. Obviously, American manufacturers can have high productivity and low wages—can have their cake and eat it too—

by turning to the Mexican Third World labor pool.

The notion that Third World wages mean lower productivity is false on its face. A 1991 Economic Policy Institute report shows that low productivity is not necessarily typical in low-wage economies. The maquiladoras, foreign-owned plants in Mexico which manufacture exclusively for export (the Hermosillo Ford plant is an example), combine Third World wages with First World productivity. It is interesting that Japan, which has been adopting robotic production systems at a rate comparable to any other economy in the world, was among the first nations other than the U.S. to invest in maquiladoras.

While Hermosillo Ford employees are among the best paid labor in Mexico, most of the half-million maquiladora workers earn less than sixty cents an hour. Women and children are preferred workers. Labor unions are no problem. Occupational safety and health are blithely ignored. As for the environment, it can look after itself.

A big reason U.S. industrialists desired a Mexico free trade agreement was to prevent possible expropriation of their plants by the Mexican government. This assurance was essential for large scale investment to proceed. Until NAFTA they had been reluctant to venture beyond the maquiladora zone, a 200-mile swath of northern Mexico. Now they can operate throughout the country. Relocation costs are quickly recovered with exploding profit margins assured by slave wage labor.

Even before NAFTA the Mexican state of Yucatan spent big money advertising: "When the U.S. is too expensive and the Far East too far, 'Yes You Can in Yucatan'." In Yucatan "Labor costs average under $1 an hour including benefits. And the employee turnover rate is less than 5% a year."

The Mexican ruling oligarchy has almost absolute power throughout the country. Workers need government approval for strikes and collective bargaining. When Mexican Volkswagen workers went on strike without authorization, all 14,000 plant employees were dismissed and the union was abolished. Officials of the reconstituted union accepted, without workers' approval, a new contract which cut the number of union stewards from 200 to 14. In the final settlement, 1,200 workers were not rehired.

The Wall Street Journal surveyed 455 corporate executives and found that fifty-five percent of them intended to shift at least some of their production to Mexico if NAFTA was approved. Mexican labor policies were a big reason. One-fourth of executives polled also admitted that NAFTA would strengthen their position in reconciling American workers to pay cuts—another tremendous motivation in the campaign for a U.S.-Mexico free trade agreement.

In *The Endangered American Dream*, author Edward Luttwak explains what a U.S.-Mexico common market would do to American workers: "If the profuse abundance of Mexican labor and the meager quantities of Mexican capital are both added to American labor and capital within a common economic zone, the total supply of labor will have increased much more than the total supply of capital. With capital now more scarce and therefore more valuable as compared to labor, the earnings of U.S. capital will greatly increase . . . The earnings of Mexican labor will also increase somewhat . . . But the earnings of American labor must greatly decline . . ."

Mexico had 90,000,000 people in 1990, with a southern border as porous as our own. An immense industrial reserve army of unemployed millions from South and Central America exerts unending downward pressure on Mexican wages rates. So even if millions of Mexicans leave their country for the U.S., Mexican wages are not affected. Millions come to replace them.

The maquiladoras have depressed U.S. wage levels. By

1986, per capita incomes in the Texas communities of Brownsville-Harlingen, Laredo and McAllen-Edinburg-Mission were less than half the national average. Even Las Cruces, New Mexico, and El Paso, Texas had per capita incomes that were, respectively, 65 and 65.4 percent of the U.S. average. More free trade will only make it worse. Eventually workers throughout the industrial Midwest, in places like Detroit, Cleveland and Pittsburgh, will find a shrunken, lower wage job market with a larger percentage of lower paying service jobs.

Free traders say we are moving into a services-oriented "technetronic age." This means that America began as an agrarian economy, then developed a balance of manufacturing and agriculture and moved on to a mix of manufacturing, services and agriculture, and will advance to an ultimate fourth stage where the services sector will employ more people than any other. Presumably the U.S. will be such a skilled services provider that no other country will dare challenge us on that front.

Yet service jobs do not pay manufacturing wages and are not immune to export themselves. California's Silicon Valley has long been the world's largest computer software producer; but as of 1994 it was second to Bangalore, India where software engineers do the same work for a quarter of the pay.

The mass export of American jobs is not limited to simple data-entry work. The contracting out of intellectual services is coming with a vengeance. Even the most high-tech white collar jobs can be exported utilizing the emerging "Global Information Infrastructure" which Vice President Gore hails as the way of the future.

Gore says that "President Clinton and I believe that the creation of a network of networks, transmitting messages and images at the speed of light across every continent, is essential to sustainable development for all the human family." Will the American branch of Gore's "human family" suffer for the rest? Many highly educated people have been fooled into accepting this vision of technological utopia. Just wait until radiologists learn that X-rays and CAT scan imagery they interpret is sent by local HMOs to comparably educated but quite cheaper practitioners in Asia. How will U.S. aerospace engineers react when they discover that work in component design is being instantaneously sent off to comparably educated, less paid engineers in China?

Some economists predict that personal servants—Jeeves the butler!—will return to homes of the elite and upper middle class. While this type of work cannot be exported, it is being imported en masse through out of control immigration. Possibly the butler will also serve as security guard—finally, protectionism for hearth and home!

Replacement of manufacturing employment with service jobs further widens the gap between rich and poor. As wage levels sink, the demand for commodities will follow. Lower commodity prices will largely benefit those who can afford them in the first place, reinforcing a vicious downward spiral. Again, the eighty percent of employees who are nonsupervisory blue and white collar workers will be hardest hit. Declining living standards will dip even further. This process unchecked would hand us a Third World economy under the thumb of a filthy rich elite. This would cause a slide into working poverty for millions. Already an ugly sign of this is the appearance of huge masses of homeless people on American streets.

Every day more and more Americans become employees of foreigners and globalist Americans who might as well be foreign (they couldn't care less about this country). Free trade dollars spent on cheaper foreign goods come back home to buy up choice U.S. businesses and real estate. Japanese conglomerates have bought American film studios, expensive downtown real estate, banks and even Rockefeller Center. Foreigners also use free trade dollars to buy steel mills along the Great Lakes, ranges of timber, ranches, farms, hotels and resorts throughout the country.

The selling off of America is not limited to major metropolitan areas. On election night 1992, supporters of President-elect Bill Clinton gathered in Little Rock in the shadow of the city's two major hotels, one of which is owned by Japanese, and the other by citizens of India. Did the celebrating Friends of Bill realize that in cheering a supporter of free trade, they were cheering on the process of their own dispossession? Did the people at Bush headquarters have a clue they were pushing the same?

Actually the Republican party has a worse record supporting free trade than the Democrats. It was House Republicans that provided Clinton with the NAFTA margin of victory. The GOP, which has won many an election on patriotic rhetoric, always talks a good game. Do they confuse patriotism with profits for multinationals? Or do they care about patriotism at all when it conflicts with transnational money-making?

The latter is a good guess. Listen to the President of NCR in 1989: "We at NCR think of ourselves as a globally competitive company that happens to be headquartered in the United States." When Saudi Arabia's Prince al Waleed bin Talal invested $590 million in Citicorp, America's largest bank, their executive vice president bleated: "We don't view ourselves as just a U.S. bank. The fact that the guy happens to be Saudi is neither here nor there."

Other corporate leaders speak of the "inevitability" of declining American wages. Goodyear Chairman Robert E. Mercer says, "Wages overseas will come up, but one way or another, the gap will have to close." Walter Joelson, head economist at General Electric, suggests, "Let's talk about differences in living standards rather than wages. What in the Bible says we should have a better living standard than others? We have to give a bit of it back." Even more blunt was the CEO of International Harvester who said he saw "no reason why the American worker should earn higher wages than the Mexican worker."

There are a few patriotic American corporate leaders who want to stop so-called free trade from destroying our industrial base. Milliken Company (textiles) CEO Roger Milliken has been quite active in efforts to spread the truth about free trade. But he is vastly outnumbered—financially a member of the elite but culturally not of it. Milliken's desire to protect the U.S. job base is outmoded thinking to the greedy elite and flies in the face of New World Order "globalism."

More in line with today's elite is Caterpillar CEO Donald V. Fites who said in 1991 that "There is a narrowing of the gap between the average American's income and that of the Mexicans. As a human being I think what is going on is positive. I don't think it is realistic for 250 million Americans to control so much of the world's GNP." Mr. Fites *claims* to be an American (as well as a human being). As CEO of one of the largest heavy equipment manufacturers in the world, Mr. Fites will not miss a meal anytime soon, but apparently could not care less if an American worker does. If you care to take issue with Mr. Fites, he can be reached at Caterpillar Inc., 1000 North East Adams Street, Peoria, Illinois, 61629. Wonder if the workers at Caterpillar know what is playing in Peoria these days in the boss' office? How about the workers at Goodyear, General Electric or International Harvester? Do they understand what is *really* endangering their livelihoods (greed) or have they swallowed the "postwar boom" or "services economy" or "globalism" or "free trade" propaganda—or all of the above?

A cold indifference to nationality leads a growing number of the very wealthy to abandon U.S. citizenship for refuge where taxes—especially estate taxes—are lower. By 1994 reported offshore accounts held by Americans from Zurich to the Cayman Islands amounted to over $2 trillion. After moving assets, the next step is often new citizenship. An attorney for the class of new expatriates explains, "You can pretty well negotiate your own private agreement with a Swiss canton about your annual income taxes." Another well-heeled expatriate voiced the sentiment, "The country in which I will be a citizen will be the one which does the most for me." This is a far cry from "Ask not what your country can do for you, but what you can do for your country."

Free trade is in fashion for political extremists. The lassiez-faire/libertarian crowd (who call themselves conservatives) see evil only in uncontrolled government (i.e., government that does not do their bidding). Leftists/Marxists (who call themselves liberals) see evil in nationalism and unfettered free enterprise. Free trade suits them both. The responsible middle ground would be to encourage the pursuit of economic gain as long as it is fair to the entire citizenry and benefits the nation as a whole. Like fire, government and business can be helpful servants—or fearful masters. Runaway big business/big government rule must be replaced by genuine Representative Government.

Big media deception has convinced many Americans that so-called "liberals" are antagonistic to multinational corporations and free trade. Greed has no political label. There are some filthy rich radical liberals around. Just look at Wall Street and Hollywood. Karl Marx, godfather of today's liberalism, favored free trade because he believed it would destroy the "chauvinistic" differences among cultures and nations which he believed stood athwart the final triumph of world Communism (or did he say corporatism?). While the Communist movement failed to eradicate cultural and national identities, free traders are doing a good job with their forced "free movement of labor and capital." The "free" movement of cheap labor accelerates the Third Worldization of America. International "free" movement of capital accelerates its sell out. This makes a lot of money for some people. Some of the former 1960s radicals are among the most greedy today—a subject which certainly begs further study.

Despite free trade, nation-states still remain the basic units of economic life. Professor John M. Culbertson in his book, *The Dangers of "Free Trade,"* presents an interesting scientific view. According to Culbertson, sociobiology has "disclosed that the higher animals achieve limitation of their populations and preservation of their habitats through arrangements that are territorial, that associate a particular group with a piece of territory . . . The group that permits overpopulation and destroys its habitat and its food supply does not survive; the group that limits its population and protects its habitat thrives, and becomes the pattern-setter for the species. The popular ideas of 'one world,' and 'abolition of all boundaries and all groups' thus clash not only with the lessons of economic experience but also with the logic of . . . living things in general."

Senator Russell Long of Louisiana rebutted Henry Kissinger's free trade yappings at a 1976 hearing: "If we trade away American jobs and farmers' incomes for some vague concept of a 'new international order,' the American people will demand from their elected representatives a new order of their own, which puts their jobs, their security and their income above the priorities of those who dealt them a bad deal." The 1994 elections showed that Americans are fed up with New World Order politics as usual. Representative Government may yet return to our land. Free trade would be its most prominent casualty.

The situation will get worse before it gets better. The

propaganda battle over NAFTA showed that we have much work ahead. Practically every Chamber of Commerce, civic club, church group and college campus was deluged with clever pro-NAFTA propaganda. Middle American resistance was not effectively mobilized. Ultimately a truly bipartisan coalition of liberal Democrats and conservative Republicans in Congress passed NAFTA on a so-called "fast track," a piece of parliamentary legerdemain which severely limits debate.

Soon after NAFTA enactment, America's favorable trade surplus with Mexico began to disappear. Ross Perot and others had warned of this and were villified throughout the land for doing so. From January through May 1994, the U.S. shipped a grand total of 16,957 motor vehicles to Mexico but imported 154,302. It is projected that Mexico will soon produce from two to three million motor vehicles annually. Since labor in Mexico costs only fifteen percent as much as labor in the U.S., it is most likely that Mexico will surpass Detroit and become the automotive capital of the Americas.

The same parliamentary shenanigans were employed to win Congressional approval of the General Agreement on Tariffs and Trade (GATT). GATT established a World Trade Organization (WTO) in which the U.S. will have no veto and will be outvoted by more than 200 to 1 by other nations. GATT not only mandates a more "free" movement of capital and goods, but also the "free" movement of cheap labor across national boundaries, an agenda fanatically promoted by former Mexican President Carlos Salinas. Scandal forced Salinas to withdraw his name from consideration as head of WTO and eventually forced his exile from Mexico. Pervasive scandal is stock in trade for the Mexican government, driving home the reality of an oversized banana republic on our southern border. Current Mexican Strong Man Ernesto Zedillo wants to use GATT to promote more labor flooding into the U.S. from his country. It is easier for peasants to leave Mexico than to reform it. Their exodus is a safety valve against popular revolution. The southern Mexican state of Chiapas is already a war zone.

GATT is even more detrimental to Middle America than NAFTA and is a wholesale surrender of U.S. sovereignty in trade policy to a world governmental body. It was passed even faster than NAFTA by an extraordinary "lame duck" session of Congress which usually acts only in time of national emergency. It was supporters of GATT who had the emergency. Again, GATT was passed on the Congressional "fast track" sham which prohibited any amendments or changes, forbade Senate filibuster, and limited Senate debate to 20 hours. In the House debate was limited to 90 minutes for each side.

A remarkable criticism of GATT, believe it or not, comes from a world famous corporate raider, Anglo-French financier Sir James Goldsmith. Goldsmith is an honorary peer, but perhaps his comments betray a wisp of genuine noblesse oblige. He warns that "Global free trade will force the poor of the rich countries to subsidize the rich in the poor countries. What GATT means is that our national wealth . . . will be transferred from a developed country like Britain . . . to developing countries like China, now building its first oceangoing navy in 500 years . . . It is quite amazing that GATT is sowing the seeds for global social upheaval and that it is not even the subject of debate in America . . . If the masses understood the truth about GATT, there would be blood in the streets of many capitals." Goldsmith's book, *La Piege* ("The Trap" in English), is a compelling expose of free trade folly.

Goldsmith also refutes David Ricardo's free trade doctrine of "comparative advantage" which urges nations to specialize in what each produces "best" and leave the rest to the free trade/free market. Along with the free trade ideas of

Adam Smith, Ricardo's "comparative advantage" now shares the ideological scrap heap alongside flat earth theory. As the appearance of land to Columbus discredited flat earth theory, the sudden appearance of billions of people on the world labor market in India, China, Vietnam, Japan, Bangladesh and the former Soviet empire did the same to "comparative advantage." A Vietnamese enterprise can employ 47 workers for what it costs to employ one Frenchman. This unbridgeable gap in labor rates explains why France's "comparative advantage" in producing a speed train for South Korea was a flop. The $2,100,000,000 contract to build the trains provided only 800 jobs in France for just four years. Most of the work is done by Asians in Asia. Following essential technology transfer, the trains will be built in South Korea and sold to other Asian nations far below prices which France could ever charge.

Third World peasant farmers simply cannot compete with multinational agribusiness conglomerates; for that reason Goldsmith believes GATT will wreak havoc when Third World agriculture collapses under the destabilizing impact of free trade. Displaced peasants will flood into cities worldwide unleashing a mass migration thousands of times greater than the movement of refugees from Rwanda, Haiti and Bosnia which has so preoccupied U.S. policy bureaucrats.

By late 1994 the U.S. was headed for the largest foreign trade deficit in its history: $160 billion. California's was more than $20 billion. Using Commerce Department ratios, this meant that California's 1994 net export deficit cost the citizens of that state a total of 400,000 jobs. New York's trade deficit, at $13 billion, has cost approximately 260,000 jobs. Not only the unemployed suffer. The downward pressure on wages and salaries resonates throughout the economy.

Further warnings about the globalist economy come

from globalists themselves. The May 1994 issue of *Populi*, a U.N. Population Fund publication, is an unlikely place to read anything that could be helpful to the United States of America. Yet in "The Long-Term Job Crunch," *Populi* admits that "We are going through the worst employment crisis since the great depression of the 1930s, according to this year's World Labor Report from the International Labor Organization . . . ILO attributes the long-term high unemployment to two trends. First, jobs have been rendered obsolete by rapid technological change—for example, the rise of robotics in automobile and other manufacturing plants. Second, the rapid movement of manufacturing capacity, capital and people in the global economy means workers in any given country now face unprecedented competition and insecurity."

By late 1994 even the Clinton administration began to re-alize that all was not well in the global economy. The December 5, 1994 issue of *Roll Call* quoted Labor Secre-tary Robert Reich as warning that "Once unbottled, mass resentment can poison the moral integrity of the nation, replacing ambition with envy, intolerance, and hate. Today, the targets are immigrants, welfare mothers, government officials, gays and an ill-defined 'counterculture.' As the middle class continues to erode, who will be the targets tomorrow?"

Well, Mr. Secretary, the targets today are Middle Ameri-cans, and you (among others) are doing the targeting. Fur-ther, Secretary Reich may be seeking a scapegoat himself by placing the blame wholly on corporations: "The Ameri-can public is basically pro-business. But that support rests on an implicit bargain. And business betrays that bargain every time it fires an older worker in order to hire a younger one at a lower wage, provides gold-plated health insurance to top executives while denying its workers health cover-age, labels employees independent contractors in order to avoid paying them full-time wages and benefits, or discards its workers rather than invest in them when profits are booming." Secretary Reich's words are 50% on the mark—he is half right. A half truth can be many, many times more devastating than a lie; maybe the good Secretary knows that. He fails (how could he?) to mention the federal government role in the Betrayal of American workers. Remember the government, the other half of the corporate welfare state? Does focusing on corporations divert attention away from that half of the problem? Is that Secretary Reich's intent? Is this part of a shell game? Isn't it big government in Washington, at the behest of multinational corporations, that authorizes free trade, NAFTA and GATT? Where was Secretary Reich during those debates? Big government and big business are in it together. They verbally attack each other for public consumption. It is a good show. It is the paramount sham. Until that important lesson is learned, Middle Americans will be hopelessly split along made to measure "conservative v. liberal" lines, which precludes effective resistance.

Remember Senator Long's putdown of big government/big business icon Henry Kissinger: ". . . the American people will demand from their elected representatives a new order of their own, which puts their jobs, their security and their income above the priorities of those who dealt them a bad deal." Let's hope Senator Long was right and that the American people do demand "a new order of their own."

Chapter Three

Foreign Aid Fiasco

Foreign immigrants invade our country. Foreign free trade dollars buy up America. There is nothing wrong with foreigners per se. There is something radically wrong with the U.S. government promoting foreign colonization of its own country. A major portion of America's resources yet to be taken over or bought by foreigners is shipped overseas as transfer payments to other foreigners. This is global welfare to foreign governments. Like our U.S. welfare programs, it engenders dependency. It is also known as foreign aid.

This most colossal scam of the twentieth century drains away billions of hard earned tax dollars. Long ago defined as "poor people in rich countries aiding rich people in poor countries," foreign aid, as it is doled out today, is a fiasco. And not all of it goes to foreigners, but to home-grown globalist parasites who might as well be aliens from afar. Parasitism begins at home, and many a high dollar Washington consultant has met his mortgage payment by "devising strategies" and "creating concepts" to "alleviate sociocultural and economic inequalities" and, yes, "reconstitute democracy" in the Third World. And these programs have had a very positive effect on the lobbyists and consultants. The Third World, democratic or not, continues to decline. And the American taxpayer continues to foot the bill for this global welfare scam.

Foreign aid is central to foreign policy, just one more

American policy where the American people don't count. Year after year American majorities tell pollsters they want foreign giveaways to stop. Yet, year after year they crop up like a hardy perennial weed. The persistence of these wasteful programs is Exhibit A in the case of the people versus the governing elite; and who do you think is winning that one?

There are really two types of foreign aid. "Direct" foreign assistance is appropriated by Congress for programs in various recipient countries. This is the more visible taxpayer rip-off, because it is actually known as foreign aid or by some other name which reveals its giveaway nature. For purposes of discussion, foreign aid masquerading as humanitarian aid, military assistance or just foreign policy is included in this more visible foreign aid.

Members of the governing elite, our "foreign policy establishment" now admit that this more direct type of foreign aid has failed, but it mysteriously breathes life anew with every Congressional appropriation. The U.S. Agency for International Development (AID) is one of the few government agencies to actually admit its own failure. On February 21, 1989 the *Washington Post* reported that AID, "after spending tens of billions of dollars in 25 years of trying to help Third World Nations stem poverty, has concluded that the program largely failed to achieve its objectives and suggested that a complete overhaul may be necessary." Despite the publication of a lengthy report with suggestions for reform, nothing was done. Four years later in August, 1993 yet another AID chief admitted that "The entire agency is on the chopping block for the vice president to look at . . . This place is a disaster."

AID, like all wasteful giveaway programs, is handed down from one administration to another. Hand-me-downs ultimately wear out—but not this one. The standard excuse for its sorry performance is that previous administrations just didn't do it right—the old partisan blame game. Appointees may come and go, but foreign aid goes on forever.

Some AID blunders are hilarious. They have given electric sewing machines to Egyptians who have no electricity, hand-cranked ice cream makers to desert people who have no ice, cash to oil-rich Arab sheiks with money to burn, and shipped free condoms to Third World countries where local merchants sold them as toy balloons. It *is* funny—until you remember who pays the bill.

And there are less funny disasters. A General Accounting Office study in June, 1993 reported that AID workers in Guatemala asked for $3 million to immunize children, but were sent $16 million. They asked Washington to take back the unspent funds, but Washington refused. An audit later revealed that one million dollars was missing, totally unaccounted for.

Rep. John Kasich wants to abolish AID. He told the story of how agency contractors in Rwanda sold donated food and used the proceeds to build an east to west tennis court. Upon learning that east-west tennis was no fun in the tropical sun, wayward contractors tore it up and rebuilt the court north to south—our tax dollars hard at work!

Similar episodes of theft, misfeasance, siphoning and waste of American aid dollars are legend. Bureaucrats say these stories are taken out of context, that the overall foreign aid picture should be reviewed before condemning it. Such a review nonetheless condemns foreign aid and validates the average American's view that it is a tremendous waste. Once again, the people are right. So what?

Half of the $15 billion in foreign aid dispensed during 1992 went to the Middle East, primarily Egypt ($2.5 billion) and Israel ($5 billion). This was steadily increased during the Cold War in hopes of stabilizing the region in the face of Soviet expansion. Today it is linked to U.S. military involvement in the ever turbulent region. Even with the

Cold War behind us and the Soviet threat diminished, secular and religious strife, Arab-Israeli problems and petroleum politics dominate the region. Each week brings news of continued strife. What has changed? The lessons learned from our domestic social welfare programs—that simply throwing money at a problem will not solve it—should perhaps be applied to our foreign aid programs as well.

Sub-Saharan Africa is another area receiving a disproportionate amount of aid, almost $2 billion in outright American largesse in 1992. President Bush introduced hundreds of millions more into the picture through the U.S. military "relief" mission in Somalia. His successor, President Clinton, similarly involved the U.S. military in Rwanda (not to mention Haiti in our own hemisphere). This kind of foreign aid is not called foreign aid because it comes out of the Defense budget. That kind of aid puts American lives at risk. And it is insane. No reason for this intervention even remotely related to U.S. national interests has ever been offered—just New World Order talk. Our young soldiers are asked to put their lives on the line for food shipments in Somalia, political campaigns in Haiti, U.N. convoys in Bosnia. They are sent to protect the borders of Kuwait when our own borders are not protected.

The combined gross national product of all sub-Saharan Africa (except South Africa) is not as much as that of tiny European Belgium. Africa is abysmally poor, though its inhabitants range over some of the richest natural resources on earth. It is also the area with the world's highest birthrates. The population of sub-Saharan Africa is growing faster than any population in history. At the same time, per capita incomes in black African nations fall precipitously. There is no limit to the amount of "relief" and "emergency" aid which the U.S. could pour into unending African strife. It is simply throwing good money after bad.

Democratic government has collapsed in one African nation after another. The last democracy to fall was Liberia in 1981. Where so-called democracy does exist in Africa, it is usually a rubber-stamp parliament packed with the leader's political cronies. Some of the despotisms in Africa are truly grotesque. President-for-life Jean Bokassa of the Central African Republic made himself Emperor Bokassa of the Central African Empire and spent tens of millions of dollars on his coronation, replicating that of Napoleon. It was calculated that the festivities consumed one-fourth of that country's gross national product. The atrocities and mass murders perpetrated by Bokassa, Idi Amin of Uganda, Colonel Mengistu of Ethiopia, Francisco Macias Nguema of Equatorial Guinea, Mobutu of Zaire and innumerable other military-backed despots in Africa are practically beyond belief.

V. S. Naipaul, a Hindu novelist born in Trinidad, has quite a reputation for his incisive analyses of the Third World. In *A New King for the Congo: Mobutu and the Nihilism of Africa*, Naipaul relates how Mobutu murdered over a million of his hapless subjects shortly after seizing power in 1965, and so consolidated his control that he remains in office thirty years later.

Robert Klitgaard, an official of the International Monetary Fund, tells the gruesome tale of Nguema in his aptly-named book, *Tropical Gangsters*. A third to one-half of Nguema's subjects in Equatorial Guinea were either murdered or driven into exile.

In Uganda approximately 200,000 people were slaughtered by the dictator Idi Amin, including schoolchildren. In the five years following Amin's departure, between 300,000 to 500,000 people in Uganda were massacred in tribal and political conflict. During that time a freezer was discovered containing the heads of decapitated Amin opponents. The late Jeffrey Dahmer's cannibalism which so shocked America was more than occasional fare in the Amin household. All this occurred in a nation of only 15 million people. Jean Francois Revel tells the story in *The Flight From Truth* and blames European nations who legitimize African tyrants. For example, France always conferred diplomatic recognition on the murderous tyrant Bokassa.

An excellent analysis of the growing Africa disaster is "The Coming Anarchy" by Robert D. Kaplan in the February, 1994 *Atlantic*. He confirms that belief in juju and the practice of polygamy remain all-important factors in African life. Naipaul and Klitgaard also present evidence of black Africa's widespread cannibalism.

Joe Wright's book, *Blood Secrets*, describes the chilling rituals of human sacrifice and cannibalism which are central to the juju religion. One episode recounts "The Two Hundred Cuts," a juju ritual wherein a kidnapped white man is literally cut two hundred times as a blood sacrifice to bestow juju power on a Nigerian leader.

Africa apologists argue the region's problems are a legacy of European imperialism or some vaguely defined racism. Even if it is all true, why are our tax dollars involved? Whatever does this have to do with us? America has no colonial obligations. The U.S. colonized only Liberia—with emancipated American slaves. The former colonial powers do not dole out aid on the scale of American largesse. The legacy of colonialism in Africa—or Africa, period—is not an American problem.

The road to hell is paved with good intentions; foreign aid to the developing world is a case in point. Former Mauritius Peace Corps worker Diana Walstad says that aid coupled with Africa's runaway birthrates only makes it worse. She wrote in the Raleigh, N.C. *News and Observer* that: "The average number of births per child-bearing woman in Ethiopia is 6.7 (compared with 1.8 in the United

States). Perhaps with media appeals and food relief, we can keep these 6.7 children alive. But when they reproduce, as they surely will, can we rescue the second generation? The third? Even countries of great wealth and benevolence cannot support forever a constantly increasing mass of human flesh; it is just not possible."

Africa's problems are endemic in the Third World. Just look at Haiti. In 1994 America became ensnared in Haiti's internal affairs at the behest of the Congressional Black Caucus. Two centuries of uninterrupted chaos and tyranny will not end with American occupation, but that is no guarantee millions will not be spent trying. One suggestion from the Black Caucus was for the United States to annex Haiti as a commonwealth similar to Puerto Rico. The last thing in the world our country needs is another overcrowded welfare paradise. Puerto Rico would have attained independence long ago but for its many "American"-owned factories (free traders, no doubt). At last count a majority of Puerto Rican households received food stamps.

In spite of all these outrages, it is the less visible type of foreign aid that is by far the most scandalous. And that is a massive sleight of hand operation which never appears as foreign aid in the federal budget. It is a taxpayer-gouging, earth-enveloping shell game running in the hundreds of billions of dollars. It bleeds American taxpayers, enriches the super rich, and rarely helps anyone who really needs it in the poor countries involved. This is international finance, a grand old scheme where the U.S. government "forgives" Third World debt while American tax dollars make good on it. It works like this: 1) the U.S., through the World Bank and International Monetary Fund (IMF), guarantees multinational bank loans to developing countries; 2) these loans provide the developing country money to subsidize multinational corporations moving in to set up cheap labor operations; 3) then foreign aid to the developing country is used to pay interest on the international bank loan which subsidizes the multinational corporation; 4) after everyone gets their cut—banks, corporations, Third World potentates, foreign aid consultants, etc.—there is usually no money left, so the developing country threatens default on the U.S. guaranteed loan; 5) to avoid default, the developing country's bank debt is partially forgiven by the guarantor (Uncle Sam). This partial debt forgiveness enables the developing country to resume interest payments on the all important loan. Should the developing country ever be completely out of debt, interest payments would end. That would not be good for the banking business!

The World Bank and IMF manage the entire process. The World Bank asks the U.S. government for loan guarantees to developing countries; the actual loan funds help the client country increase productivity so it can generate tax revenues to service its debt. *That* is why it must be productive! The IMF role is to help the debtor nation pull it off (debt service). Favorite mechanisms are to design austerity programs and "free market" reforms. Only banks and client governments come out ahead.

All was well until a mid-1980s "debt crisis" occurred. Third World debtors threatened to default en masse on liabilities totalling $1 trillion dollars. The powers that be stepped in to head off the crisis. Big media told us that adjustments to the international regulatory apparatus (World Bank/I.M.F) were made to preclude a future occurrence. No doubt it had a hefty price tag. A rational policy would be one of gradual disengagement at both ends. First, stop milking American taxpayers for all this. Second, face reality: the Third World will always be the Third World and will never function culturally, commercially or otherwise like the West. With these two simple steps, everyone would ultimately be better off. This expensive charade should be brought to a close before it collapses and takes us with it.

The dominant role of international bankers in U.S. foreign policy is nothing new. After World War I, England and France owed tremendous debts to U.S. banks. Then the Treaty of Versailles was written saying Germany owed tremendous "reparations" to England and France. None of these countries could pay. Never fear, said the bankers. They aggressively peddled German bonds to the American public. The proceeds, less fees, went to Germany so it could pay England and France which could in turn repay the U.S. This scheme worked so well that other bonds of lesser developed countries were marketed in the same way. By 1933 $25 billion of these bonds were in default; i.e., they became gifts from the American public (in the midst of the Great Depression) to foreign countries. This was a catastophe for many. Needless to say, the banks came out way ahead. However, the tyranny of debt, especially in Germany, only fueled resentment of America and international finance.

After World War II opportunity struck again—for the banks. After their lobbyists secured U.S. foreign aid to newly independent Third World regimes, they would turn around and loan money to them. The foreign aid secured their interest. The Soviet threat played right into their hands. We just had to prop up the Third World—primarily Latin America, Africa, the Middle East, and lest we forget, Vietnam—to save them from the Soviets. Foreign aid is good for business—the banking business.

And whenever conventional foreign aid was not enough, special arrangements were made. An incredibly sweet deal was the Panama Canal treaties. The corrupt government of Panama had overextended itself in commitments to New York banks. So the Panama Canal treaties were devised whereby the United States would relinquish sovereignty over the Canal Zone, and in so doing pay the government of Panama incredible sums as operating fees for the Canal. This money would enable Panama to pay off the banks.

There were stipulations in the treaties making sure the banks got theirs. A Jimmy Carter-appointed chief negotiator for the Panama Canal treaties was one Sol Linowitz, board member of Marine Midland Bank, a Panama creditor. When this outrageous conflict of interest was exposed, Linowitz grudgingly stepped down from Marine Midland's board. Nonetheless, the international banking lobby gained two-thirds approval of the treaties in the U.S. Senate while the American people were overwhelmingly opposed! The Panama Canal Treaties were sold to the American people as foreign policy—they were simply a dressed up big bank bailout.

Could the bankers top that? Say hello to the so-called Mexican "peso bailout." Mexico spent down its reserves by $13 billion and sold bonds valued at $28 billion to prop up its economy with a wildly overvalued currency. This was done to buy time for the ruling PRI party to win re-election, and for NAFTA and GATT to pass the U.S. Congress. Soon afterwards those bonds, known as tesobonos, came due— $28 billion worth. The financial community knew there was no way the government of Mexico could make payment. But not to worry—the U.S. taxpayer could be counted on to pick up the slack. The leaders of the political class in Washington—Bob Dole, Dick Gephart, Newt Gingrich, Bill Clinton—immediately banded together to sail it through Congress. Then they hit a snag; even Congress would not fall for that deal. Facing popular resistance on Capitol Hill, Democratic Treasury Secretary Robert Rubin and Republican Federal Reserve Chairman Alan Greenspan put together a $49.8 billion bailout package, signed off on by the President. Who got bailed out? The bondholders. Who are they? Out of $28 billion in bonds, one billion were held by Japanese investors, twelve billion by Mexican interests, and the remainder had been underwritten by mostly New York-based banks. Goldman Sachs, the largest underwriter of the worthless Mexican bonds, was on the hook for $5.17 billion. Who was the chairman of Goldman Sachs until Bill Clinton was elected? Robert Rubin—at $25 million a year. No wonder Rubin was installed as Treasury Secretary just weeks before the Mexican bonds came due! Not a whimper of conflict of interest allegations was seen in the mainstream press. Big media had done its job well. After all, didn't they tell us it was a "peso" bailout?

Since the rank and file of Congress balked, President Clinton ordered the Treasury Department's Exchange Stabilization Fund gutted of $20 billion to cover the high dollar bond holders. Only weeks later the dollar—once the world's strongest currency—fell to post-World War II lows against the Deutschmark and the Japanese yen. The international banking gravy train alone may drive the United States into financial ruin. Our hard-earned tax dollars, in the tens of billions, transferred Mexico's bad debts to the American taxpayer. Where in the Constitution does it say our government is in the debt consolidation business?

The results of the so-called Mexican bailout are: 1) Goldman Sachs' $5.17 billion, Citibank's $2.9 billion, J. P. Morgan's $2 billion and Bear Stearns' $1.81 billion are safe; 2) rich Mexican and Japanese bond holders were made whole; 3) the Mexican peso is worth 55% of its former value; 4) Mexico is in economic depression; and 5) the American taxpayer is committed to $49.8 billion for making it all happen.

These shenanigans are not referred to as "foreign aid" by either big media, big government, big banks or any other branch of the ruling elite; the American people were told it was all in the interest of "hemispheric security." Our border with Mexico is anything but secure, and the American dollar is well on its way to glorified peso status.

The next time you turn on the radio or television and hear talk of foreign aid, military assistance, or humanitarian aid, grab your wallet. And then ask how any of this is connected to the vital interests of the United States of America. Then *diligently* inquire as to—and it takes work—just who benefits? And who does not? As we enter the next century, what is the foreign policy of the United States? Aside from bank enrichment, it is a blend of blundering and waste, of politically correct intrusions and giveways sanctioned by occasional United Nations blessing. The vast majority of Americans are vehemently opposed to our young men and women placed in harm's way under the command of foreigners for some United Nations "mission"—another surrender of sovereignty to a world governmental body. Are international banks, oil reserves or special interests involved in these "do good" adventures? In all of the confusion, no one in U.S. government has been heard to ask what American objectives might be other than for Uncle Sam to serve as world wide charity for the suffering masses of planet Earth. And the suffering masses are always the very last to be helped—if at all.

Long after the Cold War's demise, old policies of buying friends and buying off enemies continues. What is the point of it all? The lesson here is that money talks, and U.S. taxpayers are good for it. American national interests do not count. As of early 1995, several hundred thousand American troops were stationed throughout Europe and Asia providing a security shield for our Cold War allies. More than 6,000 were in Haiti; 3,500 in Panama; approximately 2,000 throughout the former Yugoslavia; 8,000 plus throughout the Middle East and 2,600 in Somalia (still). At the dedication of the Korean War Memorial in Washington, President Clinton said that American troops will remain in Korea ". . . as long as the Korean people want them there . . ." What might the American people want?

While America's so-called leaders continue to be preoccupied with Africa, Haiti, the Middle East and China, the

European Community grows ever stronger. Three-fourths of the U.S. population is European American; and it makes sense for America to forge closer cultural and economic links with Europe. The U.S. resurrected Europe from the wreckage of World War II with the Marshall Plan, and now much of Europe has higher average living standards than America. World War II and the Cold War will be just hollow Pyrrhic victories unless our so-called leaders turn their focus toward Europe—not Asia, not Africa, not South America. In the Europeans most Americans will find kindred spirits and rational partners and will perhaps see a mirror image of themselves. The windfall profits from Third World financing are easy money in the short run for a corrupt elite; solid cooperation with Europe is the best long-term foreign policy for the vast majority of hard working, law abiding Middle American taxpayers. And it would certainly save us a few dollars in foreign aid.

Chapter Four

Immigration Warfare:
The Deadliest Deception*

Big business wants it for cheap labor. Big government wants it for a client base. Big religion wants it for new members. Big media and their politically correct running dogs in academe want it to remake America in their own multicultural image. Liberal politicians want it for more votes and more money. Conservative politicians want it for more money and more votes. Lawyers love it because it is great for business.

What we are talking about is immigration, or rather the current immigration policy which is destroying America as we know it. All of the above-mentioned elite special interests crave power, and massive immigration is a way to get it.

The American public does not want it—too bad. They are dispossessed anyway. Of all the treachery a ruling elite could perpetrate against the American people, our current immigration policy is the most virulent. If we had been commissioned to write a script for the destruction of our country, out-of-control immigration would easily suffice.

For thirty years our elected "representatives" in Washington have gone out of their way to promote an avalanche of Third World immigration to our country. While the din of do-gooder rhetoric against poverty, disease and crime resonates from Washington, our rulers do their utmost to import it. If we want a Third World country, we should just import Third World people. This policy is a lethal weapon against the American majority, for if continued there will soon be no majority. The common-sense view of most people—that immigration should be limited to reasonable levels—has been ignored by politicians showering the public with half truths and lies to conceal their betrayal agenda.

Today's immigration problem started with the Immigration Reform Act of 1965 which eliminated the restrictive national origins quota system that had been America's entirely reasonable immigration policy since 1921. The national origins system stemmed the tide of immigration that threatened to overwhelm America in the early 1900s. It was designed to preserve America's European-based ethnic composition by limiting the percentage of immigrants from each country to that group's percentage of the U.S. population. That way future immigration was compatible with the existing population, thereby preserving a "peaceable body politic."

The 1965 law was originally touted as a modest adjustment to the "discriminatory" national origins system, and a way to treat all prospective immigrants equally, no matter what their country of origin. Supporters promised the new law would have no significant impact on either the total number of immigrants or the ethnic character of the nation. They had to know better.

Hawaii's Senator Hiram Fong said that under the new law, Asians would never surpass one percent of the U.S. population. Senator Fong said: "I just want to make this point because the argument that the cultural pattern of the U.S. will change needs to be answered. Our cultural pattern will never be changed as far as America is concerned." Senator Edward Kennedy, who is still in Washington, righteously agreed. He was a leading booster of the new bill.

These assurances were patently false. Third World chain migration (immigrants sending for relatives who send for their relatives) caused a legal immigration explosion from an average of 252,000 per year in the 1950s, to around 600,000 per year by the mid-1980s. There was a limit on immigrant visas, and those few desiring to come here from Europe did not have a horde of extended family desperate to chuck it all just to be in America. But just about everyone in the Third World would come here in a heartbeat. As a result, Latin American and Asian immigrants with their extensive extended families were handed all the visas, thereby crowding out potential European immigrants. By the 1980s 45 percent of legal immigrants were Latin/Caribbean, 40 percent Asian, and less than 10 percent European. By the mid-1980s around 250,000 legal Asian immigrants entered every year. In 1960, Asians were less than one-half of one percent of the U.S. population. By 1990, they were 3 percent, and had become the majority in such places as Monterey Park, California. Hispanics are coming in at such a rate that they will soon supplant blacks as the largest minority group in America.

The elite knows this, but they want cheap labor. The American majority desired no major changes in our country's ethnic character. For that they are called racist.

Despite Mexico's generous immigration quota, illegal Mexican immigration grew exponentially from the late 1960s. Mexico's population jumped from 34 million in 1960 to 72 million in 1980. By 1995 it surpasses 90 million. In 1975 Immigration and Naturalization Service (INS) Commissioner Leonard Chapman warned that "illegal immigration is out of control." Millions of illegal aliens had crossed our southern border, but Congress refused to give the Border Patrol sufficient manpower to cope with the problem. Some years later President Reagan himself said "We have lost control of our borders." Still nothing was done.

The illegal alien invasion begun in the late 1960s continues. 86,597 illegals were apprehended in 1964; 345,353 in 1970; 766,600 in 1975; and 1,183,455 in 1985. After 20 years of ignoring desperate pleas for help from the Border Patrol, and opinion polls showing overwhelming majorities of Americans for a law against hiring illegal aliens, Congress did nothing until 1986.

What they did in 1986 was worse than nothing. The Immigration Reform and Control Act of 1986 (IRCA) offered legal status (amnesty) to millions of illegal aliens who had intentionally violated the law by coming here in the first place. Aside from rewarding the lawbreakers, IRCA did outlaw knowingly hiring illegal aliens (employer sanctions) and also committed to hire approximately 1,500 more Border Patrol officers.

Most Americans favored employer sanctions and more Border Patrol; they opposed amnesty. Self-appointed Hispanic leaders had an exactly opposite view, opposing employer sanctions while clamoring for amnesty. Congressional leaders of both parties said amnesty was the compromise necessary to win enough votes for sanctions and more Border Patrol, which they did. To make a long story short, the amnesty came about, but effective employer sanctions and more Border Patrol did not.

Amnesty was opposed by Americans for Immigration Control, the American Legion and the Veterans of Foreign Wars. They forcefully pressed the case that amnesty was rewarding lawbreakers, encouraging even more illegal immigration, would eventually cost the taxpayers billions, and would mire down the INS with paperwork.

Congress listened to the special interests. Agribusiness wanted a huge pool of cheap immigrant labor. Hispanic pressure groups wanted a larger bloc vote. Some religious organizations argued that the U.S. should be turned into a kind of worldwide "sanctuary."

An attempt to remove amnesty from the bill failed by a

vote of 199 to 192 in the House of "Representatives."
Among conservatives who voted for amnesty for *illegal*
aliens were Congressmen Jack Kemp, Newt Gingrich, Bob
Dornan, Robert Michel, Vin Weber and Senator John
McCain. Amnesty had bipartisan leadership support. It was
not a liberal v. conservative issue, but one of ruling elite v.
We the People.

So Congress solved illegal immigration by declaring it
legal. What a sham! Yet the major news media
eagerly trumpeted the lies. Millions of illegal aliens
received amnesty, the opportunity to bring in relatives, and
welfare rights. The American majority got an immigration
invasion and more lies about curbing further immigration.

Agribusiness lobbyists knocked out provisions for effective employer sanctions and obtained a separate amnesty
for farm workers who had worked as little as 90 days in the
year preceding IRCA enactment. Congressional sponsors
said that no more than 250,000 illegal aliens would apply
for this amnesty, but 1,300,000 applied, the majority with
fraudulent applications. Eventually 905,000 illegal aliens
obtained farmworker amnesty leading to U.S. citizenship.
Many of them had been nowhere near a farm.

Hispanic groups pressured Congress to add "anti-
discrimination" clauses to IRCA which made it *a federal
offense to prefer U.S. citizens to aliens in employment.* That
was an affront to common sense; but special interest elites
demanded otherwise.

In the year of IRCA's enactment, the Border Patrol
apprehended a record 1.6 million illegal aliens. The following year apprehensions dropped to 1.1 million, only because amnesty had legalized most of the former illegals.
Once 3 million amnesty claimants had their "papers," they
were no longer illegal and could stay here and cross the
border at will. It was soon common knowledge in Mexico
that employer sanctions were a farce, easily evaded by

fraudulent documentation.

The INS and Border Patrol knew employer sanctions had failed, but Congress assured us they had taken care of the problem. IRCA authorized 1,500 additional Border Patrol officers, but for eight years Congress refused to appropriate money to actually hire them. In 1993, Congress finally agreed to fund 600 additional Border Patrol agents. Eight years after IRCA became law, there were only 3,300 Border Patrol personnel on the Mexican border. At best that is 1,100 per eight hour shift—counting desk jobs—for over 2,000 miles of border.

In 1991 more than 1.8 million foreigners became legal residents of the U.S., a record year. 1.12 million were amnestied illegals. More than half (946,167) came from Mexico. Their relatives south of the border didn't waste any time packing.

In November, 1992 the Commission on Agricultural Workers, created by IRCA, reported the law was a failure. Illegal immigration was not affected. Americans throughout the southwest didn't need the federal government to let them know. An avalanche of illegal farm labor flooded the market and depressed wages. Widespread fraud and lax enforcement made the law a complete farce.

As hundreds of thousands of amnestied illegals became eligible for relief, California's welfare costs exploded. In 1992 Los Angeles County saw a 29 percent rise in welfare costs in just eighteen months.

Congress refuses to authorize computerized citizenship checks on prospective employees. The technology is there, but greedy employers and Hispanic pressure groups block it. The INS is provided neither money nor manpower to save American jobs from illegals. In Los Angeles approximately seventy INS personnel monitor approximately 500,000 businesses!

As expected the 1986 law vastly increased chain

migration. Politicians referred to amnesty as "bringing undocumented workers into the mainstream"—more politically correct bunk. The 3 million amnestied lawbreakers were quickly replaced by an even larger wave of illegals.

The 1990 Immigration Act was another sham, dramatically increasing legal immigration in the face of massive evidence that hardly any Americans favored any increase whatsoever. Passing Congress with scant media attention and virtually no public support, it was pure special interest law. The *New Republic* noted the "1990 law increasing the annual legal quota by 40 percent passed almost unnoticed" as Congress raced to adjournment.

Congressional debate on the bill was revealing. Supporters listed special interests favoring the bill, while opponents noted that the American public simply did not want any immigration increase. Overwhelming public opposition was ignored while supporters trotted out the tired old "immigration made America great" saw for window dressing. Rep. Charles Schumer (D.-N.Y.) said that: "immigrants are good for America. . . . We are a growing country, and we need more immigrants." Rep. Hamilton Fish (R.-N.Y.) explained that the bill "addresses three great areas of legal migration: family unification, diversity and employment-based immigration." Selling out Middle America is a bipartisan endeavor.

While the 1990 bill escaped mainstream media analysis, leading newspapers did endorse it. *The Washington Post* (liberal) urged Congress to hurry and pass the bill before it adjourned. *The Wall Street Journal* (conservative) called it the best Democratic bill they had seen in years. Richard Riscavage, deputy director of the U.S. Catholic Conference, let the cat out of the bag when he admitted that: "There is no question that if we hit a recession next year, the American public isn't going to want to be hearing about more immigrants. The time is ripe for a bill now."

Congressional justification for the special interest law was an exercise in deceit. The increase in "skilled workers" from 54,000 to 140,000 per year was deemed essential due to "shortages" of engineers and scientists. In April, 1992, a congressional subcommittee finally heard testimony revealing that claims of an impending shortage of scientists and engineers were absolutely false! In fact, *there is widespread unemployment among American engineers*. Big business simply wanted cheaper foreign employees, and they wanted them here. And big business gets what big business wants.

The anti-European bias of the 1965 immigration law virtually cut off immigration from Italy, Ireland, Poland and other European nations. This bias could have easily been corrected by changing the quota system under which Third Worlders hog almost all available immigrant visas for family chain migration. But Congress was not about to be fair to Europeans (not enough cheap labor, bloc votes or welfare constituencies); they just added new "diversity" numbers on top of the existing quotas. Then they turned around and dramatically increased the number of "family reunification" visas to encourage more Third World immigration. This was done to "relieve visa backlogs." How increasing immigration will reduce visa backlogs is a mystery. Immigrants who join relatives here send for more relatives—and there is a practically endless supply of these folks throughout Asia, Africa and Latin America. The *Washington Times* reported in 1993 that the visa backlog "soared 16 percent last year to nearly 3.4 million people . . . All of this follows three years of record immigration, 1989 through 1991."

President Bush signed the 1990 immigration bill on November 29, 1990, saying that "immigration reform began in 1986 with an effort to close the back door on illegal immigration and now we open the front door to increased legal immigration." Certainly "we" did not include the overwhelming majority staunchly opposed to increased immigration! When politicians say "we," look out. They don't mean "We the People," but "We the selfish and short-sighted ruling elite."

Thirty years of legislative sleight of hand are now apparent. The flood of illegal immigration is now a full-fledged invasion, a colonization, as millions cross our borders with impunity, adding an estimated 500,000 permanent residents to the U.S. population each year. Legal immigration has been increased to 900,000 people per year, triple the pre-1965 level. Visa backlogs reach into the millions. The system has just about completely broken down.

Despite assurances by big business bullhorns telling us that "immigration is a free lunch" for America, real wages for working Americans have been falling for more than twenty years. Almost 40 million people live in poverty, 10 million are unemployed, cities are overcrowded, air and water increasingly polluted, and schools overwhelmed by non-English-speaking students. California teeters on the edge of bankruptcy. There is no way its economy can withstand the cost of providing services to the vast population of legal and illegal aliens. It has joined several other states in suing to force the federal government to foot the bill for failing to enforce national immigration law.

The U.S. population is growing faster than any other industrial nation, driven by massive immigration and the high birth rates of Third World immigrants. From 179 million in 1960 to 260 million in 1994, America grew at a rate of 2,700,000 a year. In December, 1992 the U.S. Census Bureau discarded earlier population projections for even higher growth forecasts with no end in sight. The *Washington Post* admits: "Illegal immigration remains high . . . Over time, the effects of immigration on population are multiplied by higher birth rates among immigrant groups." With no change in immigration, the U.S. population will skyrocket to 392 million or more by 2050. Rocket scientists are not required to see what this will do to the quality of life in America. The very last thing America needs is more immigration.

The ethnic makeup of our country is being drastically changed. In 1960 America was 88.6 percent English-speaking whites, now known as "Anglos." By 1980 Hispanics were 6.4 percent of the population. In 1993 "Anglos" were 75 percent of the U.S. population, Hispanics 9 percent, Asians 3 percent, blacks 12 percent. As of 2053, whites will be a minority. Hispanics will be 21 percent of the nation's population, Asians 10 percent—if current immigration patterns continue. A look around the world from Bosnia to Canada suggests that unending ethnic strife will be the outcome of this rapidly changing ethnic mix. The contrasts between homogeneous Sweden or Japan and "diverse" Bosnia or South Africa speak for themselves.

Third World colonization of the U.S. is well under way. The English language and American culture are under unremitting multiculturalist attack. Lies taught to European American children are that the Founding Fathers were evil racists ("dead white males"), that American society is inherently unjust to "people of color," and that freedom of speech for Americans must be curtailed to satisfy the demands of Third World colonists and multiculturalist elitists. Immigrants are even entitled to Affirmative Action preference over native-born Americans in employment and education. Immigration advocates lied that Third World newcomers would assimilate "just like earlier immigrants." Now the lie is that we must change our country from top to bottom to placate and appease the various alien cultures.

The number of U.S. residents for whom English is a foreign language jumped by more than a third in the 1980s to 32 million. A multicultural school curriculum proposed by New York State is a good example of anti-American multiculturalist propaganda: "African Americans, Asian Americans, Puerto Ricans/Latinos, and Native Americans have all been the victims of an intellectual and educational oppression that has characterized the culture and institutions of the United States and the European American world for centuries . . ."

What will our country be like with an extra 135 million or more people? Our cities would most likely resemble places like Mexico City, Bombay, Lagos and other urban sprawls packed with tens of millions of people struggling to survive. The Hispanic poverty rate in America is 29.3 percent compared to 12 percent for European Americans. Immigrant earnings and education levels have been falling for over 20 years due to the Third World bias of the 1965 Immigration Act.

A report by Rice University economist Donald Huddle (1993) exposed the enormous cost to taxpayers of importing a welfare class—an insane idea on its face. The poverty rate of immigrants is now 43 percent higher than that of native-born Americans. Programs used and abused by the newly imported welfare class include food stamps, AFDC, public housing, free medical care, bilingual education, etc. Net costs to the American taxpayers over the next ten years will be $67 billion every year, and rising.

A California Auditor General's report (1992) estimates that illegal aliens are costing the state $3 billion a year. The number of immigrants receiving Supplemental Security income grew by an astounding 370 percent between 1982 and 1992. The "family reunification" immigration law is used by immigrants to enroll elderly parents who have never paid a cent into the system.

Yet the political elite claims we cannot afford a few thousand extra border guards. We can't afford not to hire them. Every dollar to reduce illegal immigration would ultimately save the taxpayers thousands of dollars. As the old saying goes, "An ounce of prevention is worth a pound of cure."

California today is what America will be tomorrow if immigration continues unchecked. California's population grew by 6.1 million in the 1980s, almost 40 percent from immigration. In 1991-92 the state gained at least 303,000 immigrants while experiencing a net loss of 41,000 Americans who fled to other states. Unemployment is high; the state treasury is empty, and the Third World pours in, more than happy to get menial jobs and welfare far superior to their existence back home. The wealthy work and play behind private security systems with their immigrant nannies, gardeners and maids. A Third World-type society of a very rich, self-serving elite surrounded by masses of uneducated, subsistence-level workers is emerging in Los Angeles and many other areas of California. Forty percent of Los Angeles' residents were foreign-born as of 1990. Middle class Americans flee to other states, or see their quality of life deteriorate every year. *Newsweek* (1993) summed it up: "By the year 2010, southern California will have become a Latino subcontinent—demographically, culturally and economically distinct from the rest of America." Militant Hispanics already demand secession of the southwest U.S. and its reunification with Mexico.

Immigration is driving Americans out of California, New York and other heavily impacted areas. University of Michigan demographer William Frey foresees an America of contrasting regions, some Third World, others remaining largely European American: ". . . America [is] becoming more polarized."

With world population exploding, the "push" factor in immigration grows while the "pull" of low wage jobs and easy welfare continues. World population has grown from 2.5 billion in 1950 to 5.3 billion in 1990 and is expected to reach 8.5 billion in the next 30 years. Most of the increase is in poor Third World countries. We don't need it here.

There is considerable alien involvement in criminal enterprises. Twenty-six percent of U.S. federal prison inmates are foreigners, mostly illegal aliens. During the 1992 Los Angeles riots, over sixty percent of those arrested were born outside the United States.

Today, half of California's farm workers are illegal aliens—and rising. IRCA has been a complete failure. There is so much alien labor that *The Economist* reports: ". . . typical pay has fallen from $5-6 an hour to the state minimum of $4.25 or less . . . Encouraged by the fall in wages, growers are shifting to labor-intensive crops like strawberries." Instead of mechanizing, growers are "Mexicanizing."

The American people have never wanted an immigration invasion. In 1990 when Congress increased immigration by 40 percent, only 9 percent of the people were in favor according to the Roper poll. As Congress debated amnesty for illegal aliens in 1985, a Media General-AP poll found only 34 percent supporting it, with a majority desiring to send illegal aliens home. In 1965, the year it all started, a Gallup poll showed only 7 percent of Americans for more immigration.

The elite exploits these immigrants for personal gain while setting them up as scapegoats for the problems unlimited greed has set in motion. Big media tells us "immigration built America" so they can have their cheap labor, servile servants and expanded consumer markets. They alternatively remind us of the problems caused by immigrants in order to divert attention from their own sordid machinations. It is a very clever ruse, using the immigrants as pawns in the larger cultural and economic war on majority Americans. Too many immigrants cause problems; the greater problem is the forces which benefit from the invasion.

Most Americans have opposed uncontrolled immigration all along; but recently the issue has taken on unprecedented urgency. How many more World Trade Center bombings, L.A. riots, bankrupt state governments, criminal gangs and outbreaks of tuberculosis do we need for our elected "representatives" to take action? Polls now show that more people than ever want immigration substantially reduced or halted altogether.

The solution to illegal immigration is well known. Take 10,000 National Guard, Army or Marine troops and assign them to assist the Border Patrol temporarily while new agents are trained to triple the Border Patrol's pitiful 4,600-person force. Change the law so that state and local law enforcement officers can make arrests for immigration violations, not just a few INS personnel. Impose a modest border-crossing fee. This would pay for the increased Border Patrol even before savings in the billions were realized by getting illegals off the welfare rolls and putting Americans back to work. Institute a tamper-proof Social Security card or a call-in system to make employer sanctions work. The essential technology is readily available. Shift two thousand federal workers from make-work to the real work of enforcing employer sanctions on businesses that intentionally hire illegal aliens. Fines collected could easily fund enforcement. Impose small fines on illegal aliens caught with cash in their pockets to help fund regaining control of America's borders and to discourage illegal immigration. Deny all welfare benefits (public housing, food stamps, etc.) to aliens. People shouldn't be allowed to come here—legal or illegal—to go on welfare.

Reduce legal immigration to the historic average of 300,000 per year—with no exceptions, divided between real political refugees and self-supporting, law-abiding immigrants from all nations. Change the laws to bar any alien who has violated U.S. immigration laws; clean up the ridiculous situation where so many so-called "legal" immigrants from Mexico are already here illegally when they get their visas. With all these changes, enforced, America would still have the most generous immigration policy in the world.

Our immigration problem is a result of one thing: bad public policy. This policy is about power—pure and simple. Our demographic core—Middle America—is under attack. If the big government/big business ruling class can have abundant cheap labor and unending ethnic tumult, no force can arise to oppose them. "Divide and Conquer" will have won.

Just whose country is the United States of America? Contrary to the defeatist, self-serving assertions of a corrupt ruling elite, Americans *can* control their national borders and save their country. A Third World America is not "inevitable" *if* the American majority stands up for itself and tells the political class behind our betrayal that the day of reckoning is nigh; that Representative Government is back; that we simply will not take it any more.

*The authors gratefully acknowledge the assistance of Palmer Stacy in researching and writing this chapter.

Chapter Five

Who Values the Family?

Talk is cheap; and talk about "family values" is flat out disgusting. Name a politician who is not for family values. Name one who is for drug abuse. The very first refuge of any vote-seeking weasel these days is to scream family values, which have far outpaced motherhood and apple pie in the never ending pander for public office.

The American family is under all-out attack. Debased entertainment, a debilitating social welfare system, callous manipulation by corporations and onerous taxation are assault weapons in the arsenal deployed against the family. The real problem is a much deeper one of societal priorities. The family is no longer the focal point of life in America. Money is. Family values have been replaced by greed. The American family is the most battle scarred victim of today's greed-driven New World Order.

The days when Middle American women could stay home and care for children are gone. Women may enjoy their work, but work they must. Most do not really have careers, but like their husbands they have jobs—one inside the home and one out. This fundamental unfairness comes on top of other family pressures—confiscatory taxation, the specter of unemployment, escalating debt and the demand for employee fealty to the point where supervisors come before spouses. These burdens on the family are a product of today's skewed priorities. Is it any wonder that America is rife with domestic strife, that broken homes and broken lives grow faster than any other social phenomenon?

The double-digit inflation that rocked America during the 1970s drove millions of women into the workplace. But the necessity for dual income households did not subside with high inflation. Today the two-earner household is the norm; and one of those earners most likely has a second job as well. In August, 1994, the U.S. Labor Department reported that seven million Americans held 15 million jobs. Most multiple jobholders were married, almost evenly split between men and women.

The New York Times noted that "No other nation approaches the United States in multiple jobholders, and the clear implication of such comparative analysis, says Richard Freeman, a Harvard labor economist, is that in other countries, wages from one job are sufficient." Freeman said: "You would have thought that as women entered the work force, that would have been enough additional income, and dual job holding would have declined. Instead, the opposite has happened. Women going to work have not brought in enough income."

Older readers will remember that during the 1950s, popular media predicted that before century's end the average work week would be reduced to only 20 to 25 hours. New technology would make it all possible and increase productivity besides. With that mission accomplished, the average household would be supported by one earner with more leisure time than ever before.

Stunning technological breakthroughs continue, but the number of working hours required to support today's smaller households is way up. What happened to the great productivity boom technology promised? The average family now has less time than ever to function as a family. The home has become a dormitory for at least two workers, and children are dispatched to daycare.

Juliet Schor's book, *The Overworked American,* documents the disappearance of leisure time. Schor found that in 1994 working women spent about 305 more hours a year at their jobs than in 1969. This equals 7.5 weeks or 38 added days of work each year. Far fewer women worked full-time outside the home in 1969. Schor concludes that working women put in 145 hours less each year on domestic tasks, including child care, than they did in 1969. By comparison, working men in 1994 were spending 98 more hours at work than in 1969. And precious few of those guys had more time to help out around the house.

Children suffer most. Parents today spend 40 percent less time with their children than did parents in 1965. This catastrophe does not show up in data on declining living standards, but is a big part of it. Neither television nor day-care can replace an absentee parent. The negative impact of this forced parental neglect has a multiplier effect, weakening the social order at all points, especially by wiping out much of the continuity between generations which is essential to maintaining a stable society. "Quality time" simply cannot compensate for less time.

Rutgers University sociologist Paul Popenoe defines "the ideal child-rearing environment" as a family "that does a lot of things together, has many routines and traditions, and provides a great deal of quality contact time between adults and children; regular contact with relatives, active neighboring in a supportive neighborhood, and contact with the world of work; little concern on the part of children that their parents will break up; and the coming together of all these ingredients in the development of a rich family sub-culture that has lasting meaning and strongly promulgates such family values as cooperation and sharing."

Obviously, few families today have time for all that! The negative effect of diminished quality time is felt well beyond the immediate family. Neighborhoods suffer from the lack of interpersonal networks, leaving the streets for the delinquent and criminal. The larger community suffers from a lack of citizen participation. No amount of rhetoric about "initiative" or "a thousand points of light" can compensate for the consumption of our precious time.

It is tragic enough that surviving nuclear families have so little time together, but they are also increasingly isolated. In our essentially rootless society, the vast extended family—grandparents, uncles, aunts, brothers, sisters, cousins—is absent, hundreds or even thousands of miles away. It is difficult to realize full emotional support from an extended family scattered to the winds. Many an intact nuclear family is just two individuals marooned in a strange environment for want of a secure job.

An even greater tragedy is that almost 50 percent of families now have only one parent present in the home (U.S. Census Bureau, August, 1994). In many cases the family is no longer in crisis—it has simply ceased to exist.

The ruling elite, that top one percent owning the means of production, distribution and communication, is largely indifferent to burdens on the family. The upper five to ten percent of Americans—self-employed professionals, business owners, Chamber of Commerce types—often acquire their world view from the elite and look to the core middle class for clients and customers. They mouth compassion for the underclass from which they are insulated and offer an abundance of ideas as to how Middle Americans should live. These are the people who make sure family values rhetoric is dispensed as needed with each election.

Of course, there is no better pawn in the liberal v. conservative brawling than the beleaguered American family. Liberals rant about male chauvinism and sexism; conservatives sermonize about morality. Elitists and religious zealots suggest that women could stay home and be full-time homemakers if only they had the right "values." Both ends of the political establishment blame the deterioration of

American family life on everything but the ruinous corporate welfare state.

Working Americans know better; but are hard pressed to get the word out in the controlled print and broadcast media. Families are doing their best to make ends meet; and there is nothing fundamentally wrong with their values. It's just that Middle Americans are trapped between a greedy elite with a hand in their pocket and a criminal underclass at the doorstep.

Neither big business nor big government cares one whit. Money manipulators see no families, only robots—interchangeable economic units of production and consumption. The less individualistic, the more efficient. Transnational corporations seek to eradicate any group identity among Middle Americans which could divert them from complete fealty to market forces. Family values are obsolete—they don't make money.

This attitude comes through loud and clear in the mass media. Fortunes are made pumping explicit sex and gratuitous violence into American homes and theatres around the clock. Is this an assault on family values or what? Middle Americans attempt to combat this through all manner of protest, but nothing seems to work. If families are to free themselves from the entertainment industry squalor, they must either: 1) acquire ownership of or some control over big media; 2) patronize and support alternative media exclusively, or 3) provide their own family entertainment. Freedom begins at home. Those who complain about the amorality of television should immediately be asked two questions: "Why don't you just turn it off?" and "Would you allow an individual to enter your house, stand where the television is, and do it live in your living room?" If an industry ever set itself up for a hostile takeover, the entertainment industry is the one.

Talk radio is the only mass media outlet where Middle

America is heard. Why else would the elite call it "hate radio?" Talk radio may one day pose a real challenge to politically correct thought control. So far it is only a money making, though politically incorrect, adjunct to big media.

Churches are practically alone in expressing a genuine concern for the family. But churches run way behind the entertainment industry in their influence on mores and lifestyles. Many churches deteriorate along with the family, even offering sermons based on television programs. Congregants often drive straight from services to partake of the latest new network sitcom.

Religious leaders with mass media access regularly hold forth against the many symptoms of family decline. Ugly as they are, the problems of pornography, abortion and the "gay rights" movement are merely symptoms of the family's crisis. These problems would have never reached their present critical mass if the family had not already been driven from its rightful place at the center of American life.

Television evangelists rarely emphasize that the American family has been deprived of its vital center, the homemaker, now that both husband and wife must work full-time outside the home. They would be right on target letting their flock know that out of control greed is the primary cause of collapsing family life. Its effect has been to deny working men incomes sufficient to support their families; and it is that—not any so-called "women's liberation"—which has swept American women en masse out of the home and into the workforce. The sins of lust are bad enough, and a favorite target of preachers nationwide. But what about the Biblical injunction: "The love of money is the root of all evil?" The sin of greed is the real destroyer of American family life. Greed is the incentive for producing morally debased entertainment. If the family came first, it wouldn't happen. The sin of greed has denied men the wages and salaries necessary to support their families, savaging their traditional role as husband, father and provider. This is how greed has swept the homemaker from the home. Greed sends American jobs overseas and reduces the American standard of living in this age of plenty.

Greedy employers seized upon the women's liberation movement to reap even more profits. They have cleverly responded to the call for gender income equality by gradually reducing the incomes of men. Much of this discrimination against the male breadwinner has been carried out through Affirmative Action. And it has added a new workplace dimension to relations between men and women, putting further pressure on family relationships. Men are losing ground, and are accused of "male chauvinism" when seeking to defend their eroding status.

Both sexes are so preoccupied with their immediate problems that they don't see the forest for the trees. Multinational corporations are not concerned with stable, loving families or with families, period. What they can "bring to the table" for the corporate bottom line is important. Massive corporate transfers (much less layoffs) stress families and committed relationships to the limit. The nomadic existence of moving about like chess pieces is described as market forces in action. What about family forces? What good is a system that subordinates the welfare of families to short-term considerations of profit and productivity? Such a system is morally bankrupt and fundamentally corrupt. It is bad for families and bad for America. Let the greedy elite set up a corporate welfare state somewhere else. Greed should not rule this country. How long can any system continue if it destroys the family, the one institution absolutely essential to any society's heath and well being?

Multinational corporations don't have inheritance taxes which are often a major problem for family businesses. After all, they have great tax lobbyists. Family businesses of any significance are either going under or fast being acquired. The family business once thrived in America like the family farm, as a focus of everyday life, strength and continuity through the generations. While family-based enterprises are unlikely to return in today's economic climate, it is absolutely essential that working Americans, blue and white collar, unite and resist anti-family, corporate/government power. There is nothing unionist, socialist, rightist, leftist or radical about getting out from under tyranny. It is essential to the revitalization of family life and free enterprise. If such resistance needs a label, call it family values.

Oddly enough, the only 1996 Presidential candidate mentioning the big business squeeze on the family is a Republican—veteran big media gadfly and lapsed conservative Patrick J. Buchanan. This is an odd development in a party funded from top to bottom by corporate PAC money. Why else would talk of family values ignore the devastating impact of corporate greed?

While elite indifference towards the family is obvious, so is the threat from the growing criminal underclass. Aside from bleeding families to feed the criminal justice and welfare bureaucracies, crime ravages the American family even more. Crime takes a huge toll in community, emotional well-being, money and lives. It costs more to live in crime-infested areas and even more to get away from them.

The housing, automobile and debt industries profit handsomely from American crime refugees. For two decades suburban development in large metropolitan areas has been driven by Middle America's flight from underclass criminality. This is an unpleasant topic in politically correct circles, so people talk about moving "to a better neighborhood" or "a better atmosphere" or "better schools." Why are the schools, neighborhoods and atmospheres better? Generations ago thriving, nurturing communities flourished in the most congested of urban areas with a fraction of the financial resources available today. And all this came into being without urban renewal or affirmative action.

Fleeing the terror of urban crime has a great influence on consumer spending, considerably raising the average family's transportation and housing costs. Longer commutes mean overburdened public transit and more new cars more often. Residential real estate is not a secure investment at all when neighborhoods are invaded by the underclass. Real estate markets can be notoriously unstable. Middle Americans have more and more of their assets tied up in automobiles which depreciate every month and in home values exposed to the vagaries of social pathology and financial speculation.

Joseph Minarik of the Congressional Joint Economic Committee has calculated that the average 30-year-old man could make mortgage payments on a median priced house in 1973 with 21 percent of his gross income. By 1987 that same figure was 40 percent of an average 30-year-old's gross income. Today, most American families able to purchase a home are doing it on at least two incomes.

Much of the inflation in housing costs is generated by baby boomer demand. High divorce rates are also a factor. Yet thousands of houses in urban America stand empty or are demolished because buyers cannot be found. They are in high crime areas.

Forced to spend whopping percentages of earnings on taxes, housing, automobiles and debt service, the average family fails to adequately invest for retirement or save for emergencies. Their income is consumed to feed the system rather than being prudently invested to create new wealth. This makes it almost impossible for an American family to become financially independent.

The growth of America's criminal underclass has been subsidized by the same welfare system that finished off its family structure. Yet the underclass is much more than a crime and welfare problem. Look at what it costs the Middle American family! While conservatives rail against the government/underclass axis to pander for middle class votes, liberals fixate on supposed racism and corporate transgressions to shore up minority bloc votes. Neither acknowledges that their respective bogeymen are in it together, pressing a deadly pincer movement against the American family.

Big government's current system of taxation has made life miserable for American families. In 1950 a median-income family paid 2 percent of its gross earnings in federal income tax. By 1991 this had risen to 24 percent. Added to this were state and local taxes. *Today the average American family pays more in all taxes than it spends on food, clothing and shelter combined!* And don't forget health insurance, which has been increasing at twice the rate of inflation for a generation. Conservatives and quite a few liberals receive substantial campaign money from the health insurance industry, and that is ideology enough for them to oppose efforts for reform. Liberals are deathly afraid of a Middle American tax revolt which would endanger programs important to buying the bloc vote. Once again conservatives and liberals flog their pet scapegoats while ignoring the deeper systemic corruption.

An overhaul of the tax system is long overdue. A dramatically simplified income tax with generous personal and dependent deductions should be considered. Equitable health insurance reform would also be a boost for the American family. When people become suddenly ill or unemployed, or are denied coverage through bureaucratic chicanery, they need help. The American family has few friends in high places because it is not a source of high dollar campaign contributions, nor does it bloc vote or take to the streets—not yet.

The Great Betrayal is nowhere more shameful than in

the case of the American family. The Republican Party promises the good old days if only big business is helped. The old GOP mantra of deregulation, which sounds fair enough on its face, could possibly mean an end to Social Security, Medicare, and other programs that, when properly administered, could be of help to struggling families. But the way they are being run now assures their total collapse in a few years. The Democratic Party, beholden to federal largesse and the underclass bloc vote, carps about the good that could be done if only big government was unshackled to step in and "help" everyone. Some of their more fanatical members blame middle class families for everything from cruelty to animals to "racism." Just remember that unlike the American family, both major political parties are riding high with the current status quo.

The next time you hear we must have "compassion" for vicious criminals, that immigration is great for the economy, that globalism is the wave of the future, that we must be "tolerant" of corruption, and that the government is trying to help us, just remember the family—and how the elite has placed it a far distant second to greed.

Chapter Six

"Welfare" versus the General Welfare

To obfuscate means to render indistinct or confuse. The less distinct issues become, the more confusing they are. Mass confusion prevents a popular consensus of opinion. Large-scale obfuscation is a great way to divide Middle America.

One way big media does this is by taking well known words with positive connotations and changing their popular meaning through selective overuse. This is propaganda. There is an entire vocabulary of politically correct terminology which has come into being this way. **Welfare** is a prime example.

Welfare is the "state of faring or doing well; state or condition in regard to well-being; esp., condition of health, happiness, or prosperity or the like." The Founding Fathers desired "to promote the general welfare." This was a selfless, patriotic aspiration for the benefit of the entire body politic. It is a fundamental premise of Representative Government. It has nothing whatever to do with multimillion dollar slush funds manipulated to acquire political power and cultural hegemony—disguised as public assistance giveaways. The Founding Fathers had no idea of a welfare class or the transcontinental cesspool of waste, misery and corruption which is today's welfare system. Modern day U.S. "welfare" in practice is the exact opposite of "general welfare" as known to the Founding Fathers.

There is hope for the general welfare in our country; but

we need to look elsewhere for an example. We should simply look to those countries with programs that work. Again, it is our European partners who can possibly help. Germany is a prosperous country, the anchor of modern day Europe. Much has been written about the German welfare system, but little of it in the popular media. However, commentary in the November 12, 1990, *Washington Post* is a good point of reference. The German social welfare system works. Contrasts to the American "welfare" system are astonishing, and outlined as follows:

1) American families pay more for health insurance if they have children. Parents in the German health system do not. The German system covers virtually all costs for children, unlike private systems in the U.S.

2) German parents receive a monthly payment of 600 marks ($450) to cover the special costs of the child's first six months. These payments are received by all German parents, regardless of income.

3) German parents receive a child allowance until the child is 16 years of age. The monthly payment for three children is 260 marks ($166), an allowance which continues if the child enters the higher education system.

4) German universities charge no tuition. The need for American parents to start saving hundreds of dollars each month for college funds is simply unknown to German parents. Furthermore, this free access to higher education is not limited by parental income levels. Of course, Germany does not have a federally subsidized higher education industry on the scale of America.

5) German families with three or more children are entitled to a "family pass" (50 percent discount) for the national rail system. This benefit would not mean a great deal in the U.S. where everyone must own private automobiles.

6) Middle class German families pay about $600 a year for child care for a four-year-old. Comparable cost in the

U.S. is $4,000. Additional children are cared for at reduced rates.

7) German working women are entitled to 14 weeks of paid maternity leave. Time for prenatal care may be taken on work time. The mother's job is safe for one year after her child's birth.

8) German families receive much greater income tax deductions for children than American families. German parents receive a $1,000 deduction per child per year for eight years if it is used to build or buy a house. While Americans often delay having children in order to buy a house, the German family finds that having children helps them to buy a house.

Most remarkable about the German welfare system is its equality. It is extended to all parents, rich and poor alike. It is a form of state reinforcement for intact families, not just for so-called "broken homes" or households which were never whole families to begin with. By encouraging families to stay intact through enabling mothers to care for their own children while fathers work, the German system actually promotes the general welfare of Germany.

How is such largesse possible? At first glance, the German system of family support seems much too costly for adoption in the U.S.

Low German birth rates are a significant factor that makes the German system financially possible. Why are American birth rates so much higher? Middle America's birth rate has fallen to below replacement levels, no higher than the German birth rate. The higher American birth rate is due to much higher birth rates among the underclass, which practically monopolizes social welfare in America. Not only that, the American welfare system subsidizes the higher welfare birthrate and taxes productive Americans to support it. Another factor in America's higher birthrate is the large number of births to illegal aliens. In his open letter to the President of August 10, 1993, Governor Pete Wilson of California noted that "Two-thirds of all the babies born in Los Angeles County public hospitals are born to illegal immigrant parents."

"Welfare" is now a significant part of American life. It affects everyone. By late 1993, 14 million Americans were enrolled in "welfare" programs. This was 2 million more than in 1989. By 1992 more than 9,126,000 children were enrolled in Aid to Families with Dependent Children (AFDC). As of 1991 there were 68,527,000 people resident in the U.S. who were 18 years of age or younger. The total percentage of children in AFDC far exceeded the percentage of U.S. households enrolled. (See *United States Statistical Abstract, 1993*, tables 16 and 604.)

So while only 7 percent of American households were on AFDC, they accounted for almost 14 percent of the nation's children. The average "welfare" household has well over twice the U.S. average number of children. The cost of maintaining these households was $210 billion in 1990, up to $240 billion in 1991 (Congressional Research Service).

Although the poverty rate has risen only slightly, welfare spending as a percentage of GNP has risen from 1.5 percent when Lyndon Johnson launched his War on Poverty in 1965 to 5 percent in 1994. In 1965 Johnson announced that "the days of the dole in the United States are numbered." Thirty years later they certainly are, one way or another. The money is running out.

If $240 billion (5% of GNP) isn't bad enough, that is only part of it. AFDC's hidden costs to society are incalculable, but are no doubt several times what shows up in federal and state budgets.

One way to consider AFDC's hidden costs is to look at three societal groupings: 1) those who solve society's problems; 2) those who sustain society; and 3) those who create problems for a society. The American welfare class is a problem, and it creates problems. And our welfare system does its utmost to increase the problem and finance its expansion. Middle America is a problem solver by virtue of its stable, productive and orderly character. America's leadership elite has become largely self-serving. So the very group with the greatest resources to do something has abdicated any problem solver role and pursued an agenda of greed. That development alone is a problem that inevitably compounds itself.

Today the very welfare system, created to solve problems, is a major problem itself. It has evolved into a program of institutionalized dependency. Its major mission is to protect and grow its client base, the welfare class. One welfare program after another has turned into a bureaucratic nightmare efficient only in perpetuating misery.

In 1974 Congress passed the Supplementary Security Income (SSI) program. It was established to help the blind, elderly or otherwise disabled through income supplements. But then social engineering intellectuals prevailed on Congress to "extend" the definition of "disabled," much as the definition of welfare has been changed. Now "disabled" officially includes drug addicts and alcoholics—it's the law. Even pamphlets have been distributed in urban areas asking: "Are you an alcoholic or a drug addict? Then you may qualify for SSI." According to a recent report on television's *60 Minutes* program, many SSI recipients have their checks mailed directly to liquor stores. A clever tactic of big government in these times is to create more and more protected classes of people in the name of equality. Forget about protection for Middle America.

The food stamp program is another cauldron of corruption. Begun with a minor appropriation as a Great Society initiative to prevent malnutrition, by 1994 the U.S. Department of Agriculture (USDA) was spending $24 billion on food stamps for more than 26,000,000 Americans.

By that time USDA's Food and Nutrition Service had only 46 personnel to police the program. The Secret Service reports that illegal trafficking in food stamps may surpass $2 billion a year. In September, 1994 federal authorities in New York busted 60 people allegedly involved in "laundering" $40 million in food stamps. Like AFDC, the full extent of the problem is anybody's guess. In some inner city areas, food stamps are treated like a second currency, undermining the hard earned currency of Middle Americans. There are even counterfeit food stamps in "circulation."

In the face of widespread food stamp theft and fraud, USDA awarded $2.5 million to 27 community action groups to publicize food stamp availability. Rather than trying to get people off welfare, this is a cozy tax-funded endeavor to shore up the food stamp client base. When the new Republican-led Congress made a great show of moving to kill the food stamp program, it was big business—agribusiness and grocery chains—who stepped in and saved it. Lickspittle Congressman backed down rather than incur the wrath of their patrons. Big business and big government were once again on common ground.

Another problem creating initiative is Medicaid funding of infertility treatment for AFDC mothers. In Massachusetts, of 260 Medicaid patients receiving infertility drugs in 1993, 58 percent were on AFDC and 63 percent were already mothers! Despite publicity (*Newsweek*, April 4, 1994) most such programs were still in place by 1995. Fertility drugs often cause multiple births, so we are indeed paying for multiplication of the welfare class. Meanwhile, Middle American families enduring the heartbreak of infertility must pay in the thousands for such treatments, very often not covered by health insurance.

"Parents Crazy for Federal Cash" (*Newsweek*, Oct. 31, 1994) exposed yet another welfare scam, so-called "crazy checks." These go to families with children not behaving in "an age-appropriate manner." The number of these SSI checks went from 296,000 to 800,000 in only four years. At least 750,000 other requests were rejected in the previous two years—not crazy enough. Finally, the skyrocketing number of SSI recipients with supposed behavioral disorders triggered a Congressional investigation. Many parents were coaching their children to "act crazy" when investigators appeared so Uncle Sam could cut them a check. It is the welfare system that is crazy.

In the early 1990s, collecting "crazy checks" was a major growth industry in the impoverished Mississippi Delta. In the Delta counties of Arkansas, eligibility for "crazy checks" shot up from 1,746 in December, 1990 to 4,359 in December, 1992. Mississippi County took honors; their "crazy check" recipients jumped from 198 to 702. Throughout the Delta investigators found that parents were coaching children to misbehave in school or fail tests in order to qualify as developmentally disabled. The most commonly claimed disorders were attention-deficit syndrome, hyperactivity, and similar pathologies often difficult to diagnose.

Horror stories about welfare mothers have become such stock in trade for conservative politicians that they are often dismissed by weary voters (politicians *are* known to tell a good lie now and then). But on occasion such outrageous cases come to light that not even big media can pass them up. An example was one Eulalia Rivera, a Puerto Rican immigrant living in Boston public housing. By two husbands she gave birth to 17 children, 14 still living in the U.S.—all on welfare. Ranging from their early 20s to 48, virtually none of Eulalia's children had full-time jobs and few graduated from high school. Her 17 children produced 74 grandchildren, all coming of age in the welfare system. 15 great-grandchildren had arrived as of the February 20, 1994 *Boston Globe* article, so a fourth generation is on welfare. Annual cost to taxpayers for the whole family is approximately $1,000,000.

Time reported another horror headlined "Calcutta, Illinois." It described the plight of 19 children abused and abandoned in Chicago public housing. President Clinton has suggested that people such as the Rivera family and the abandoned Chicago children represent "the outerclass," a group of people even more detached from the larger society than is the underclass. Whatever you call them, they are the Third World in the United States of America—and we pay for them to have more and more children.

There are literally millions of such stories, costing taxpayers an arm and a leg in welfare benefits. Remember the real cost of welfare in America goes way beyond five percent of GNP. The cost is many times greater because the entire welfare system is designed to promote the problem, which is the breeding of a larger and larger underclass client base which will wreak havoc at every level of society.

AFDC is the best example of a program diametrically opposed to its original purpose. AFDC was founded in 1935 to enable widowed mothers to stay home and take care of their children. The "Report to the President on AFDC" said it was "designed to release from the wage-earning role the person whose natural function is to give her children the physical and affectionate guardianship necessary not only to keep them from falling into social misfortune, but more affirmatively to rear them into citizens capable of contributing to society."

In other words, AFDC was originally intended to function not unlike the German child welfare system. But it eventually became a support system for families consisting of mother, children and state, with husband and father intentionally excluded. The government is now the sole family breadwinner. AFDC's original purpose of enabling wives to be full-time mothers has been abandoned. It now enables unmarried women to be full-time mothers. Our welfare system's message is that the government will provide women benefits only if they have at least one child, do not work, and do not marry the father. It rewards sloth and illegitimacy, pure and simple. And it doesn't do much for family values.

AFDC would be a terrible enough problem if it merely undermined the family. It also has the dubious distinction of increasing the ranks of the criminal underclass. While welfare spending has increased eightfold since 1960, crime rates have tripled. Welfare is not a deterrent to crime at all. In fact it has the opposite effect.

The controversial book by Charles Murray and the late Richard Herrnstein, *The Bell Curve: Intelligence and Class Structure in American Life*, presents extensive evidence that crime, poverty, and welfare dependency are linked to low intelligence (or I.Q.) levels, that low intelligence is predominantly inherited, that persons of low I.Q. are outbreeding persons of high I.Q., and that measures should be taken to limit the proliferation of low-I.Q. people in the U.S. population. A lengthy section of the book presents data showing that welfare mothers produce a hugely disproportionate number of low-I.Q. illegitimate children.

A touchy issue which rears its ugly head whenever serious welfare reform is discussed is race. While a narrow plurality of those receiving some welfare benefits are white, a grossly disproportionate percentage of the welfare underclass is non-white. Beneficiaries of the current system are ever ready to hobble serious discussion by rousing that tired old bogeyman: racism. If proposed reforms or get-tough measures can in any way be linked to racism, they are dropped like a hot potato. The welfare lobby has no problem playing the race card to get out the vote: keep those cards and letters coming to Congress! This foments hate— the last thing we need—in a population already wracked by criminality, poverty, illegitimacy, and a host of other social pathologies. Hate begets hate, racial or otherwise. And it is well known that a generous amount of it exists in the welfare underclass. This hatred is no doubt a factor in underclass criminality, yet welfarecrats play it for all it is worth, so our tax dollars end up subsidizing hate. Could that be a hate crime?

By 1994 the U.S. illegitimacy rate had risen to 26 percent of all births. A majority of the children born to women on welfare are illegitimate. Does this explosion in single motherhood represent a crisis in values, or is it simply a latter day life-style option for young women? In inner cities the overwhelming majority of births are to single mothers.

There is plenty of talk about welfare reform. In the 1988 election campaign we were told that pending reforms would require welfare recipients to work. By 1992 only one percent of AFDC parents were actually required to enroll in "workfare."

It is doubtful that workfare will benefit either the taxpayer or its participants. According to the Congressional Budget Office, workfare would not be a money-saving measure. *The New York Times* reports this is because "the average mother with two children receives $4,440 a year in welfare benefits. But the budget office estimated that enrolling her in a work program would raise the figure to $11,440 a year, adding $4,000 for wage subsidies and for supervisors' salaries, and $3,000 for child care."

Workfare, like job training programs, will not be effective if full-time jobs are not available. Creating jobs is a daunting task, but it must happen for people to overcome welfare dependency. Welfare reform advocates often fail to look at the larger context, assuming the larger economy will somehow take care of it. Social engineers are rarely known for practical thinking.

Professor Virginia Abernethy of Vanderbilt University

Medical School has written an excellent article: "To Reform Welfare, Reform Immigration," *Governing* (August, 1994). Dr. Abernethy cites numerous statistics relevant to welfare reform: First, the U.S. Department of Health and Human Services has estimated that 2.3 million net new jobs are needed to move present welfare recipients into the full-time work force. Secondly, the U.S. Immigration and Naturalization Service issued 1.3 million work authorizations in 1992 and estimated that another 300,000 illegal entrants took jobs that same year. The U.S. economy created 2 million net new jobs in 1992, but with 900,000 native-born Americans entering the work force, there was still an acute job shortage.

Given the U.S. government's own statistics, Dr. Abernethy asks why so many immigrants are allowed to enter the country. She points out that the U.S. labor surplus affects even the most educated. Ph.D.s in engineering, mathematics and the physical sciences experience difficulties in finding work, so millions of Americans are actually underemployed, most of them native born.

Abernethy calls for immigration to be reduced to 200,000 people annually because: "A pause in immigration would let welfare reform proceed smoothly. The market could absorb the unemployed, reenegage the discouraged worker and relieve the welfare burden. A genuine labor shortage, if it materialized, would encourage a substitution of technology for labor, enhancing productivity and leaving room for noninflationary wage raises."

In late 1994 House Speaker-to-be Newt Gingrich suggested that children of dysfunctional families and incompetent welfare mothers could be placed in orphanages. Apart from humanitarian considerations, that idea seems like an invitation to begin just another costly program. And there is no guarantee that welfare mothers would stop producing offspring for a revived orphanage industry.

The goal of true welfare reform should be to stop the breeding of a welfare class. Should welfare mothers who persist in bearing illegitimate children be denied benefits? Serious humanitarian questions are involved. Is it right to let children suffer for the irresponsible deeds of their parents? Would such a sanction be a sufficient deterrent?

An effective remedy for irresponsible welfare mothers might be to treat them as we do delinquent fathers. Men who refuse to pay alimony or child support can find themselves in jail. Such a threat to welfare mothers who persist in having children at taxpayer expense might work. However, despite all the clamor for gender equality, this is one measure of equality unlikely to ever come about.

Statutes regarding bastardy (to call illegitimate fatherhood by its old-fashioned name) have not been enforced in decades, but advances in DNA identification could make it feasible. A new movement to make men responsible, using modern technology to enforce it, should find favor among feminists.

At the very least, unmarried welfare mothers should not be rewarded for having more children. As the welfare class expands and becomes more desperate, there will be increasing calls for abstinence, birth control and other programs to curb the high birthrates. It will no doubt be argued that such measures would be a cost-effective expenditure of government funds, giving welfare mothers their choice as to method of birth control. Norplant is an easily implanted contraceptive device, effective for several years. While reprehensible conduct may be a way of life for the underclass, government promotion of this blight on our country is downright criminal.

The welfare system ravages an entire class of people through chronic dependency and then does its utmost to increase their numbers. It pays for laziness and illegitimacy while penalizing initiative and morality. The American "welfare" system is at war with the general welfare. Unlike the German system which rewards responsible, legal parenthood, it taxes responsible people to reward irresponsible illegitimate parenthood. Middle American taxpayers must often postpone having children of their own in order to satisfy the taxes and other economic burdens of the corporate welfare state, including the out-of-control welfare programs.

Is that a hate crime against Middle America? It is not necessarily a conspiracy. But it is ample evidence that the U.S. is run by an elite which lacks the will to govern responsibly and shifts the burden of its failures onto productive and law-abiding Middle Americans.

Chapter Seven

Crime, Guns and Criminal Politics

Crime is tearing our society apart. It has done more to change the way people think, act, live and treat one another than any social phenomenon. This section does not focus on the pervasive corruption known as white collar crime, but on that most visible and deadly type of crime that has taken over our streets, besieged our homes, endangered our families and ravaged our wallets.

Crime statistics are often distorted to reassure the public. The only sure thing is that crime is out of control. The ruling elite offers no relief. The treatment of crime makes money; its cure would not. The only protection we may have is ourselves and whatever we can pick up in a hurry.

Big media has put guns at center stage of the crime issue —a masterful deception. So if you talk about crime, you will be talking about guns, one way or the other. To do something about crime, we must do something about not guns, not automobiles, not spaceships, but criminals. Criminals are not guns. Criminals are people too.

Examining the American crime situation is a daunting task. Crime statistics are meaningless unless considered in their historical context. A look at New York City from 1944 to 1994 reveals just how far America has regressed to some terminal stage of criminal anarchy. In 1944 New York City had 150,000 more inhabitants than it does today. Migration to the suburbs is a major reason. So-called urban renewal has helped. In 1944, 97 percent of all children born in New

York City were born into two-parent families. In 1994 it was 50 percent. In 1944, 100 babies in the city were sent to orphanages. In 1994 thousands of babies were abandoned, many showing up in trash cans. Most telling of all, in 1944 a grand total of 40 people in New York City died of gunshot wounds. In 1994, 40 people were shot to death every ten days. (Family Research Council; July, 1994 *Imprimis*)

The New York City of 1944 seems almost idyllic in contrast with the Third World hell that is New York City today. What happened to bring about this transformation? Did the people living in the city change in some way? How are they different today than they were fifty years ago? What happened to their sense of values?

Obviously there are more criminals per capita—a lot more—than forty years ago.

Even if there were no more criminals in New York City, crime would still be on the increase because criminals today are more likely to be free and back on the street to commit more crime. Nationally known criminologist James Q. Wilson in *Crime and Public Policy* (1994) explains that "The probability of being arrested for a given crime is lower in 1994 than it was in 1974. The amount of time served in state prison has been declining more or less steadily since the 1940s: the median time served for burglary, for example, was thirty months in 1945 and thirteen months in 1994 . . . Taking all crimes together, time served fell from twenty-five months in 1945 to thirteen months in 1984."

If criminals have more time to ply their trade, more crimes will be committed. And the lack of punishment tells criminal types that maybe they can afford the risk. Even if caught, they'll be out soon enough.

In addition, there is a new justification for crime that was not present fifty years ago. This new excuse is that the material wealth, the law and the people to be violated are of another dominant, oppressor society which is socially,

culturally and racially different. This is multiculturalism of
the street. While difficult enough to quantify, it is prevalent
in the hate speech spouted by criminals everywhere. Enterprising legal shysters have introduced it as a criminal defense. This sort of thinking is dangerous. Why else would
supposed "racism" even be mentioned in the trial of foot-
ball "hero" O. J. Simpson who became fabulously wealthy
in the "dominant" society? Years ago syndicated columnist
Samuel Francis wrote of "crime as social revolution." It
certainly involves some revolutionary thinking.

Criminals may or may not consciously figure the odds of
going to jail, but there is a correlation between crime rates
and the probability of incarceration. Texas A & M economist Morgan Reynolds studied this relationship over a 38-
year period. According to his research, while the average
time served decreased from 24 days in 1954 to 8.5 days in
1988, the number of serious crimes rose from 1.8 million to
13.9 million. (Average time served was low due to probation, parole, plea bargains and high numbers of at-large offenders). While the likelihood of punishment declined, the
rate of violent crimes rose from 16 per 100,000 population
in 1960 to 75.8 per 100,000 in 1992. (*CJ Weekly Report for
Executives*, 9/26/94)

New prisons were not built in Michigan from 1981 to
1986 and the violent crime rate rose by 25 percent. Michigan began new prison construction in 1986 and the violent
crime rate had fallen 12 percent by 1989. From 1980 to
1992, the ten states with the largest increase in prison populations had a 20 percent decline in crime rates. The ten
states with the least increase in prison population suffered
an average 9 percent increase in crime rates.

Texas is showing us a realistic response to violent crime.
By the end of 1995, Texas will have completed a three-year
program to build prisons with enough space for 154,000
convicts. This prison capacity will surpass that of Califor-

nia, with a much larger population. The Texas prisons will function as two separate systems; one for violent offenders, and the other for nonviolent offenders who make up 43 percent of inmates.

While prisons keep criminals off the street, they offer better living conditions than most public housing projects, diminishing their crime deterrent value. New incarceration initiatives like the revived chain gangs in Alabama add an essential punitive aspect to incarceration which may not otherwise be appreciated by hard core criminals.

Under new sentencing laws, Texas offenders will serve a minimum of half their sentence with no time off for good behavior. This tougher approach followed widespread public outrage over the case of Kenneth McDuff, who murdered three teenagers in 1966. He was given a life sentence but paroled in 1989 because of federal prison overcrowding guidelines. Law enforcement officials predicted that McDuff would kill again if released, and he did. After just three days on parole, McDuff killed the first of three more victims. As of 1995 he was awaiting death by lethal injection. Capital punishment is undergoing a revival, and if swiftly administered, is considered the most effective deterrent to crime .

Public outrage over the McDuff case caused Governor Ann Richards to reduce the number paroled each day from 150 to 63. Locking up violent offenders for longer makes a big difference. During the past two years, the rate of violent crime in Texas is down 6 percent. While nothing remarkable about that, it backs up what common sense already tells us: criminals in prison can't get to more people to commit more crimes! Perhaps a moron could understand this, but it would be quite a revelation for some legal and social services bureaucrats.

It was U.S. District Court Judge Norma L. Shapiro who ruled that prison overcrowding was unconstitutional. Her dictates imposed an eight-year "prison cap" which made it virtually impossible to incarcerate persons convicted in Philadelphia, thereby unleashing an unparalleled crime wave on the city. Princeton Professor John J. DiIulio wrote in *The Wall Street Journal* (October 26, 1994) that "In effect, Judge Shapiro has single-handedly decriminalized property and drug crimes in the City of Brotherly Love. Some 67% of all defendants released because of her prison cap simply fail to appear in court . . . in the past 18 months alone, 9,732 arrestees out on the streets on pretrial release because of her prison cap, were arrested on second charges, including 79 murders, 90 rapes, 701 burglaries, 959 robberies, 1,113 assaults . . ." Who says one person can't make a difference? Judge Shapiro did.

Dr. DiIulio says: "There is an activist judge behind each of the most perverse failures of today's justice system: violent offenders serving barely 40% of their sentences; 3.5 million criminals, most of them repeat offenders, on the streets on probation and parole; 35% of all persons arrested for violent crime on probation, parole, or pretrial release at the time of their arrest." Judge Shapiro, like all Federal Judges, is a lifetime appointee with a six-figure salary. Easy for her to just let 'em out. Most Federal Judges do not live in high crime areas anyway.

Former prosecutor Alice Vachss blames much of this on her colleagues because of their habitual eagerness to accept outrageous plea bargains. Vachss cited several notorious cases, among them that of Melvin Carter, the "College Terrace Rapist," who was allowed to plead "no contest" to 23 counts of rape, assault and burglary. He confessed to raping almost 100 women near three colleges in California. His sentence of 25 years in prison became 12 years behind bars and three on parole for "good behavior."

While Melvin Carter's case is outrageous, plea bargaining is routine. Bureau of Justice statistics say just 3 percent of all felony cases go to trial, while 97 percent are plea bargained or dismissed. Twenty-three percent of murder and manslaughter cases and only 11 percent of rape cases ever go to trial. So mandatory sentencing guidelines do not apply in the majority of violent felonies. This is because so-called "mandatory" sentencing only goes into effect when a case makes it to trial, not when it is plea bargained. Does the general public know this? The prosecutors so eager to arrange these ridiculous plea bargains are the very ones supposed to "go after" these criminals on behalf of the public. Talk about Betrayal!

One enormous difference between fifty years ago and the U.S.A. today is that in the old days convicted violent felons were given much less opportunity to reenter society and repeatedly prey upon it. Another major difference from fifty years ago is that (in both relative and absolute terms) there are many more violent criminals in our country. High birth rates of single welfare mothers and immigration are important factors.

The most shocking increase in violent criminality is among American youth, most prominently among inner city youth. The homicide rate among males aged 15 to 19 soared from 13 per 100,000 in 1985 to 33 per 100,000 in 1991—an over 250 percent increase in just six years. The epidemic of drug abuse, particularly crack cocaine, was a significant factor.

This raging epidemic of teenage homicide was part of an upward trend in violent crime. The FBI's Uniform Crime Reports graphed three major crime trends over the last forty years. The first was from 1950 to 1963 when crime rates were relatively flat. 1964 to 1971 saw a sharp rise, with rates continuing to increase until the early 1980s. In the early 1980s, there was a brief interlude—a slight decrease in violent crime, followed by another steep rise from 1985 to 1992.

The youth of these offenders brings to mind one fact from fifty years ago which seems absolutely amazing today: in 1944, 97 percent of New York City's children were born into two-parent families. Today, illegitimacy is the inner city norm, especially in public housing projects. Americans are being overwhelmed with criminals because their society deliberately breeds them under the guise of maintaining a welfare system. Furthermore, the leadership elite accepts this, either out of fear of violent underclass uprising or fear of being labeled racist. In any event the people who could most influence public policy to do something about it are the ones least disposed to do anything. They can afford expensive private security systems and safe neighborhoods. They can also afford to unleash criminals upon Middle America—it is not their problem—yet.

Large-scale urban public housing projects are a kind of sociobiological factory working at capacity to create and procreate criminals. James Bovard in *Lost Rights: The Destruction of American Liberty*, cites striking correlations between violent crime and "the projects." In Chicago's Rockwell Garden project, violent crime is so dangerous that children sleep in bathtubs to avoid stray bullets. In Chicago's Robert Taylor project, the violent crime rate is 13 times the national average. Forty percent of Boston project residents feel unsafe in their own apartments. In Washington, D.C., 80 percent of the city's violent crime is in the projects.

Bovard quotes HUD analyst Irving Werfeld: "When the urban riots of the late sixties occurred, it was more than coincidental that in many cities the centers of the disturbances were in public housing projects." Bovard also quotes George Sternlieb of the Center for Urban Policy Research at Rutgers University, saying that public housing creates "a moral and psychological bankruptcy" in its residents.

Finally, realizing the utter despair in public housing had reached its critical mass, HUD Secretary Henry Cisneros concocted a plan to alleviate the misery: dispersion, as much as possible in middle income areas. If the Clinton administration thinks they have an "angry white male" problem now, let Cisneros have his way. All Middle America needs is a peripatetic welfare diaspora invading its space—and being taxed for it to boot.

The elite, fearing underclass violence and middle class backlash, offers up half-baked solutions such as increasing the number of police rather than cutting off subsidies for criminals. So along with these totally ineffectual "crime control" measures, the establishment has opted to take the politically correct way out by creating a smokescreen to distract the public—gun control. Big media is selling gun control as crime control. Automobile control (license, registration, etc.) didn't work against drunk drivers—hard-core law enforcement does. Gun control won't work against criminals. But gun control is not about crime, it is about power. The ultimate objective of the gun control campaign is to abolish the Second Amendment. As crime continues out of control, globalists line their pockets, and the working population sinks to ever lower living standards. The elite fears an armed citizenry in the days ahead.

Why do you think that right after the Oklahoma City bombing, big media focused on a totally unrelated subject—the militias? The prime bombing suspect had only fleeting contact with any militia group; but he had strong ties to the U.S. military. The U.S. military and its massive arsenal are under firm control of the corporate welfare state elite. But the militias have guns, and are not controlled by the elite. So big media attempted to demonize law-abiding militia people to the public.

Gun control is big government at its worst. Outlawing

guns would make lawbreakers out of millions of law-abiding citizens. It would criminalize many Middle Americans. It would certainly require a gigantic law enforcement bureaucracy. Perhaps no one in public life is more aware of this bizarre combination of anarchy and tyranny than nationally syndicated columnist Dr. Samuel Francis (*Washington Times*, Nov. 13, 1992):

"Under anarcho-tyranny government fails to enforce the laws and perform the functions it has a legitimate duty to enforce and perform, while it invents laws and functions it has no legitimate duty to make or carry out. In such utopias of anarcho-tyranny as New York and Washington, government and the munchkins who run it have virtually given up any pretence of enforcing the law against the killers, muggers, robbers and rapists who haunt the streets. Instead, they devise plea bargains, paroles, therapy programs and dropped charges for hardened criminals and concentrate their energies on such crises as illegal parking and gun ownership."

The campaign to outlaw private gun ownership is hypocrisy without parallel. Not only is it hypocritical to claim the Founding Fathers said one thing and meant another, it is the utmost arrogance for today's opinion elite to second guess the founders of what (pre-Betrayal) was the most-enlightened government on earth. By claiming that the Second Amendment does not say what it says, the new prohibitionists argue that only citizens in a National Guard militia may own guns. Gun ownership, they claim, is a "collective right" limited to a formal militia organized by the state, not an individual right. Collective—sound familiar? They collect our guns, our rights, our money.

The Founding Fathers were gun owners themselves—every one—and wrote the Second Amendment to protect that most fundamental right of man, self defense. This entire book could be devoted to quotation after quotation from the Founding Fathers definitively calling for the right of individuals to keep and bear arms. Thousands had died for this right in the Revolutionary War; on numerous occasions the British colonial government had attempted to confiscate the private firearms of civilian citizens. Big media's ceaseless din of anti-gun propaganda is devoid of any references to what these great statesmen had to say about the right to keep and bear arms except to creatively distort their definition of militia.

If there is any doubt about the intent of the framers of the Constitution on this issue, read on: James Madison, who is given more credit than most for writing the Constitution, wrote in *The Federalist Papers, No. 46*, that the whole body of the citizenry must have the right to bear arms. European monarchies were "afraid to trust the people with arms."

Our country has been teeming with privately held weapons since colonial times. With the exception of an occasional out-of-the-way skid row, the downtown areas of our cities were perfectly safe to walk until the welfare class came of age. It is not the possession of guns that causes crime, but the people abusing the guns. Gun prohibition will not prevent gun abuse any more than liquor Prohibition stopped alcohol abuse—it just impinges on the rights of the law-abiding. It is a clever strategy to shift the focus of the violent crime debate away from criminals and onto guns, distracting us from doing something about the real problem. Crime is not a gun problem. Crime is a criminal problem. Let us focus on criminals—without criminals there would be no crime.

The Second Amendment was not about "Guns are only for hunting: hence, guns not appropriate for hunters may not be owned." Yet this specious logic is actually a big part of today's assault on the Second Amendment. The lessons of history are callously discarded in the effort to disarm

America.

Disarming America would be another attack on the family by taking away their last line of defense against criminality run amok. Furthermore, the Middle American male's role as provider is already just about destroyed. Gun control threatens his traditional role of family protector as well. Into the resulting vacuum would enter Big Brother—the power of the state, the governing apparatus of the elite.

Widespread private gun ownership deters crime in ways not readily apparent. Discussion about guns usually focuses on fighting off criminal attacks. The crime deterrent value of gun ownership rarely gets air time on big media. Yet many such confrontations never come about because the average criminal, realizing that any homeowner may have a gun, is reluctant to break into a place where people are present. If the day comes when private gun ownership is banned, criminals will terrorize citizens with impunity.

With a completely disarmed populace, criminal terror would have free reign until the public demanded police protection. To answer this demand, the United States would become, operationally speaking, a police state. Law enforcement officers would function as eyes and ears of the state, watching everyone, criminal or not, and reporting their activities to higher up police state bureaucrats.

Many criminologists argue that everyone is a potential criminal, that there are no hard and fast lines between criminals and law-abiding citizens. The corollary to this theory is that everyone must be watched at all times and in all places. What better way to achieve this goal than to stampede the citizenry into demanding a police state?

Dr. Samuel Francis has written: "The ruling elite is busy inventing more subtle methods of mass disarmament. There are waiting periods for buying guns. There are feel-good, turn-in-your-guns programs. There are laws banning guns for minors. There are proposals to ban or tax bullets. There is the arbitrary search of people for guns now being mounted by the District of Columbia police."

The right to carry a concealed weapon is very important. Since the legalization of "concealed carry" in Florida, violent crime has decreased sharply. The criminals don't know just who will fight back. That is why they scope out tourists in rental cars leaving Miami International Airport. They know that guns are not allowed on planes.

The right to carry a concealed weapon will have a tremendous impact on the sociology of America. Criminals would be on the defensive for a change. Fear will turn into power—and middle class citizens will be empowered to protect themselves. Private gun ownership is Middle American empowerment. What is so frightening about that?

The realities of concealed carry and the underclass criminal revolution have nullified much of the big government/big media propaganda against guns. This is not to say they will quit trying. Charges of racism, recklessness, and redneckism notwithstanding, the average American will defend themselves one way or another. They know better. This is just family values to them.

The elite simply does not respond to violent crime—but then they are rarely victims of it. As the state-subsidized criminal population grows, those who can afford it retreat further into the suburbs, wall themselves off in heavily fortified upscale housing, or withdraw from urban America altogether. The private security industry is booming. To Middle America guns are a big part of our protection. There is no reason to confiscate the firearms of law-abiding Middle Americans because of the gun abuse problem of the welfare underclass. Prohibition doesn't work. The United States is becoming more and more like a Third World country every day—culturally, socially and economically. Private gun ownership could one day be the only thing standing between Middle America and the complete collapse of public order.

Of course, the police state necessary to enforce prohibition would work out rather well for big government. As international banking scams, government waste, corruption and welfare drain our economy, further depressing the job base, a police state would be a massive government jobs program—steady employment for millions who would otherwise be pounding the pavement unpaid. By that time we would all be so beaten down that some actual sense of public order could be enforced at last. The economic world view will have completely prevailed. There would be full employment, a depressed standard of living, a disarmed populace, a sheltered wealthy elite and oppressive public order. That sounds like a hospitable climate for record corporate profits!

Chapter Eight

The Debt Bomb

I magine a huge apartment house built like a Roman temple. It shelters residents and gives them a feeling of comfort and security. Think of this house as the United States of America.

Now, imagine a time bomb quietly ticking away in the cellar, a bomb with enough explosive force to destroy the building several times over. People living in expensive penthouse suites know all about the bomb. They are not worried because they know approximately when it will go off and plan to be away for the explosion. These are today's politicians, mass media moguls and the wealthy elites they represent.

These people have deliberately not told the others who live on the many lower levels—Middle American taxpayers—about the bomb and the impending explosion. They are expendable . . .

This little parable describes what is happening today with the American economy. Important decisions are being made that benefit only the politicians, special interests and the wealthy. Their trillion dollar costs and the misery they cause are laid squarely on the majority of hard working, Middle American taxpayers. Unless the debt bomb is defused, it will eventually explode and destroy the structure that sustains America's middle class.

Thomas Jefferson foresaw the possibility of just such an eventuality. Two hundred years ago, he warned against fiscal irresponsibility on the part of national leaders by declaring that the living had no moral right to bind the yet unborn to financial servitude: "I wish it were possible to obtain a simple amendment to our Constitution . . . I mean an additional article, taking from the federal government the power of borrowing."

Gradually, years and years of small federal budget deficits have resulted in an onerous debt. When federal spending exceeds tax revenues, money to finance the difference is raised by selling Treasury notes and other securities at a fixed rate of interest. The total of these securities outstanding is the national debt.

As with any scheme of spending more than you have, sooner or later accounts must be settled. In the case of our national debt, the day of reckoning is repeatedly delayed by simply selling additional Treasury notes to pay off the ones that come due. This not only fails to resolve the problem, but it makes it worse because the interest due on the notes requires selling even more notes each year just to pay off the ones that have already come due.

This is a merry-go-round of indebtedness, growing larger with each turn because additional interest must be paid just to keep it going. None of this debt is ever actually retired; it is simply "rolled over" into new notes. To keep people from appreciating the true size and problem of the national debt, the politicians count only the interest in each year's federal budget—the notes sold to refinance the debt principal are "off-budget." So far the banks have done very well on this.

Thirty years ago interest was only a tiny portion of the yearly budget. With the fiscal year 1994 (Oct. 1, 1993-Sept. 30, 1994) budget, interest became the second largest single expenditure in the budget, after entitlement programs. Hundreds of billions of dollars in interest alone will have to be paid in fiscal 1994 —and this will only put off the inevitable day of reckoning for a few years longer.

Fed up with the fiscal, political and cultural insanity and desperate for change, sixty-two percent of voters in the 1992 Presidential election voted against incumbent George Bush. The 1992 campaign's voice in the wilderness, brave enough to address the deficit issue head on, was Ross Perot. Big media unloaded on him. From conservative Rush Limbaugh to the liberal *New York Times,* anything remotely related to Perot that could possibly be critical—from a disgruntled campaign volunteer to his very physique—was given major play. The man's selfless efforts on behalf of POWs and MIAs and the courageous rescue of his employees from captivity in Iran were scarcely mentioned. The smear campaign was ginned up again when Perot emerged as the leading opponent of NAFTA in 1993. This is what happens to even a billionaire who dares rock the boat.

Clinton moved swiftly after the election to break his campaign promise of a tax cut for the middle class. Instead, he demanded tax increases on virtually everyone above the poverty level while claiming that he was only more heavily taxing "the wealthy." The truly wealthy, of course, are not nearly as affected as Middle Americans.

As Clinton's tax program evolved into law, it became more and more apparent that the plan was a carbon copy of the fraudulent 1990 deal. The largest tax increase in history would take place immediately, and the budget cuts, if any, would come in the "out years" beginning in 1997, after the next presidential election.

Big media was strangely silent about the similarity of Clinton's plan to the previous bipartisan deficit reduction scheme. Virtually no one in the press mentioned that the fiscal year 1994 budget (enacted in 1993) was the first "out year" budget in which the real spending cuts promised by the 1990 deal were supposed to take place. Instead of cuts, massive new taxes were imposed, and spending reduction once again was delayed until after the next election.

Senator Hollings was proven correct in his assessment that "only a fool" could believe that the difficult decisions would really be made in 1993. With this in mind, can anyone really believe that 1997 will be any different?

When the phrase "deficit reduction" is used in Washington, it never means significant cuts in the deficit, but only a reduction in the rate of growth of the deficit. Under one of Clinton's plans, the deficit for fiscal year 1996 will still be more than $200 billion, a rate that will add an additional trillion dollars to the national debt every five years.

It gets worse. Clinton's figures indicated that by 1999 the yearly deficit will soar back up to around $350 billion! Even the White House admits that its "fix" of 1993 is not a real resolution of the deficit problem.

Many Americans believe that they are not directly affected by the deficit or the national debt, but they should understand that these twin problems represent a very real danger to their livelihood, stability and economic survival.

The old idea of the national debt as something "we owe to ourselves" is less true today than ever. Initially, Americans purchased virtually all of the notes financing the deficit by investing in Treasury bills, U.S. Savings Bonds and other forms of public debt. Over the years, these "investments in America" have actually hampered economic growth by diverting trillions of dollars—which could have been used to expand businesses and produce private-sector jobs—into wasteful schemes of the federal bureaucracy.

Over the past quarter-century, even the vibrant American economy has been unable to absorb the seemingly limitless ability of Congress to overspend. More and more of the Treasury notes that finance government debt are being purchased by foreign interests—Middle Eastern oil sheiks, wealthy Europeans and Japanese, multi-national cartels and other entities who do not have America's interests at heart. Although interest rates have fallen in recent years, interest paid on the notes must remain competitive for investors to buy more.

As Ross Perot pointed out, a frighteningly large percentage of the notes securing the national debt are short-term securities. If higher-paying investments become available elsewhere, the U.S. will have to raise its interest rates to entice investors back—because the simple fact is that the federal government cannot afford to redeem its notes for cash.

If no more securities could be sold, the government's entire financial apparatus would collapse like the gigantic pyramid scheme that it is. To pay even a quarter of the current $4 trillion national debt, taxes would have to be raised more than four times the amount of the 1993 Clinton tax raise, which is already the largest tax increase in the history of the United States!

Small middle-income investors would bear the brunt of a U.S. government default. These are the people who have bought Savings Bonds for more than 50 years and who put their modest retirement dollars into "ultra-safe" government securities to ensure that the money would be there for old age. Now, with the wheel of federal debt spinning out of control, these are the people most at risk of spending their declining years in poverty. Remember, these are Americans with U.S. government securities. Were they holding Mexican bonds, perhaps they could breathe a little easier.

The current national debt represents a burden of roughly $16,000 for every man, woman, and child in the country—regardless of their income levels. That figure will rise to $20,000 in less than four years, and even higher if the Clinton administration's relatively optimistic projections turn out to be accurate. These facts, which are seldom mentioned in the press, make the magnitude of the crisis clear.

A stunning example of fiscal irresponsibility was the

Senate's failure to pass the proposed Balanced Budget Amendment. In the face of overwhelming public support and a calamitous deficit crisis, the Republican leadership in the Senate allowed it to go down to defeat. Oregon Senator Mark Hatfield was the lone Republican against the Amendment which needed one more vote for the required two-thirds majority. Hatfield offered to resign from the Senate, guaranteeing its passage. If both Senator Dole and Senator Hatfield are to be believed, then Senate Majority Leader Bob Dole opted to save his buddy Hatfield's seat rather than pass the Amendment—the Washington buddy system in action. Middle America lost big on that one.

The Balanced Budget Amendment is no panacea, but would have been at least some restraint on spending. Several Senators who had pledged to support a Balanced Budget Amendment in the 1994 election did the opposite— perhaps the most glaring example is California's Senator Diane Feinstein. The balanced budget was a key issue in her very close reelection. Unfortunately, this is just politics as usual.

However, without firm tax limitation, any balanced budget initiative will not work. The size of government should be cut greatly; so should taxes. The latest ruse is to divide public opinion (divide and conquer) between "tax cutters" and "deficit hawks." The obfuscation (lie) here is that you are either in favor of cutting taxes or reducing the deficit. Both are essential for the future economic viability of our country, and both can easily be done—*if the political will is there to do it*. Doing both would reduce the deficits and increase domestic productivity.

"Balancing the budget on the backs of the poor" is another shop-worn slogan. If the fiscal insanity continues, we'll all be poor. "Piling the deficit on the backs of the middle class" is closer to the truth.

The Federal Reserve will probably monetize the debt;

i.e., just print more and more money. Of course, this is highly inflationary. A surplus of anything cheapens its value, and the U.S. dollar has been falling like a stone.

So-called economic "shock therapy" was used to wean some Eastern European countries from Communist economics. Massive spending and tax cuts would be shock therapy for the ruling elite, as both would empower the middle class.

Meanwhile, standards of living decline, the dollar weakens, and the debt time bomb is ticking away in the cellar of every American home. Average Americans want government off their backs and out of their pockets. Government spending causes taxes. Cut spending and cut taxes. If Congress is not forced to stop the reckless overspending soon, it may be too late to avoid even further economic disaster.

Chapter Nine

Government Of, By, and For . . .
The Lawyers!

W hen it comes to greed, the legal profession is right up there with the mega-interests driving America to the poor house. Matters have deteriorated to the point that the legal system exists to serve the legal industry, sometimes known as the legal profession. In this way the legal system is no different than any other branch of the federal leviathan—its back is turned on Middle America. The lawyers own it.

As a group the legal industry has done much to reduce America to a confrontational, better-watch-your-back society. Money-grubbing squabbles rule the day, and civility has practically disappeared. Shakespeare's "The first thing we do, let's kill all the lawyers" is now more of a rallying cry than a joke. Some can quote the New Testament where it condemns lawyers outright. Millions of Americans tell lawyer jokes. Thousands of Americans are part of the Quixotic pro se movement of "constitutional patriots" who seek to derail the judicial system by filing frivolous suits. One individual has even run for President as the candidate of a Down With Lawyers Party.

Popular contempt for attorneys is a quite reasonable reaction to institutionalized chicanery. The root of this widely held disgust lies with: 1) widespread litigation terrorism, and 2) the realization that our formerly Representative Government has degenerated to a regime representing lawyers and their special interest clientele.

Lawyers are the quintessential special interest group because they can write and change the rules practically at will. Many beleaguered working Americans in need of legal representation know this. They have seen the rules of their attorney's billing change overnight—usually at a critical juncture in their representation. This is such a common occurrence that an entire body of legal procedure has arisen just to handle so called "fee disputes"—so much for trust! The U.S. has seventy percent of the world's lawyers. There are more than sixty thousand members of the Washington, D.C. bar alone. The law business and its legal industry are choking America through flagrant and vicious abuse of the law and legal system. Utilizing every device imaginable, these hyper-mercenary pit bulls will stop at nothing to make a buck. Such wholesale depravity has given new life to that age-old canard—*shyster*.

America had more than 750,000 lawyers at the beginning of 1995, up from a mere 285,000 in 1960. But there is never a surplus because lawyers, unique among professionals, generate business for one another. As soon as Smith retains a lawyer to sue Jones, it means that Jones must retain a lawyer, and so forth. No other service providers—not doctors, plumbers, nor accountants—can create business for each other like this. Making money off other people's misery is stock in trade for attorneys, and the incentive is to create more misery. This self-perpetuating nature of the litigation industry enables the U.S. to support more than 300 lawyers per 100,000 people, a rate that Britain, with 103 per 100,000, does not begin to match, let alone Japan, with only 12 lawyers per 100,000 people. (Does Japan suffer in any way from its lack of lawyers?)

Civil litigation is a growth industry—14 million suits were filed in 1984; 15.5 in 1986; 16.6 million in 1990—which has the capacity to stifle and destroy individuals, firms and entire industries. Litigation in America has rocketed upward partly because losers in civil suits, unlike other countries, do not have to pay the legal costs of the winners. The defendant in a civil suit, though he may have no liability whatsoever, will often surrender his rights and settle out of court rather than face the costly and lengthy ordeal of unlimited demands for "discovery" of records and inevitable court delays. (Before reforms in Britain, Dickens made this ruinous process the theme of his satirical novel, *Bleak House*.)

Two other peculiarities of the American legal system encourage growth in litigation. Lawyers may charge contingency fees; i.e., the plaintiff only pays if they win. This encourages lawyers to direct suits at deep pockets corporations because winning one big case could mean sudden wealth virtually overnight. Contingency fees are ridiculously high, from one-third to fifty percent of the take. Another new development of the American legal system is the concept of relative liability. If a wealthy corporation is found to be even partially responsible for an injury, the take may be much larger than if the defendant were an individual found to be wholly liable.

Though it has destroyed entire industries, product liability is incredibly lucrative for lawyers. In his book, *The Endangered American Dream*, Edward Luttwak tells how the general aviation industry was virtually shut down when Cessna, Beach and Piper, the leading firms, found that their product liability costs averaged more per aircraft than the cost of building the aircraft itself. Yet despite the disastrous impact of the liability industry upon all areas of economic activity, tort reform is highly unlikely as long as the American Trial Lawyers Association remains the country's most powerful lobby and its members the largest single category of contributors to Presidential and Congressional campaigns.

Americans have come to realize that they no longer live under a government of laws. The rule of law has given way to the rule of lawyers (this includes lawyer judges, lawyer bureaucrats, lawyer elected officials). The judicial branch, by definition, is the exclusive domain of lawyers. The legislative branch, the 104th Congress (elected 1994), has 224 lawyers; 170 in the House of Representatives, and 54 (a majority) in the Senate. The executive branch is another bastion of lawyers who busy themselves by crafting thickets of entangling regulatory law which severely impede commerce. The Greeks have given the English language descriptive terms for all manner of forms of government—democracy, ochlocracy, oligarchy, tyranny, etc.—but there is no term for government by the legal industry.

Drawing on the days when the practice of law was a respected profession, many of today's greedmeisters hide behind the respectable facades of "old line" or "established" law firms where the old "respected" name remains on the door above reproach, providing cover for greed, amorality and deception practiced with calculated abandon. Lawyers work for justice much as prostitutes ply their trade for love. When it comes to charging for services, the legal "profession" has certainly stolen a march on the oldest profession. Padding the bills is just one of many ways to pad their pockets. Once a respected group in society, they are no more. An overwhelming number are individually regarded with disgust and contempt, having ousted the likes of Shakespeare's Shylock from their status as societal scourge.

Lawyers are well compensated technicians, the service corps of the elite. They benefit from elite largesse in fees, contacts, expenses and fine vacations. When the deep pockets client has a condo in Vail, Honolulu or New York, they're off. While they function as attack dogs in intra-elite disputes, the costs are passed along to Middle America and rarely affect share prices.

The ambition of most attorneys is to join the ranks of the elite, an ambition realized with disturbing frequency. Enterprising shysters accomplish this through consummate networking and multimillion dollar settlements in contingency fee cases. This is milking the big government/big business apparatus in order to climb aboard. The ultimate deep pockets target is the U.S. Treasury which can print its own money. Many a razor-sharp shyster has scored a seven figure hit under the guise of coming to the rescue of beleaguered citizens. They help mostly themselves. Aspiring to join the elite, attorneys are inveterate social climbers. Yet despite their social pretensions (a practically universal characteristic) and grandiose ambitions, attorneys for the most part are retainers of the elite much as court jesters and house servants functioned as retainers of earlier ruling classes. They even charge retainer fees. Most claw a comfortable enough existence practicing "law" by the fee honored axiom: no money, no justice.

Habitual bottom feeding is another characteristic of the legal industry. Public Defenders are paid well by the Courts to process and plea bargain underclass criminals back onto the streets, guaranteeing future business for themselves. A politically connected scavenger can live well on our tax dollars this way, and has no need to produce deceptive advertisements for his services.

The lawyer infested Congress is another focal point of popular outrage. It is not surprising that salaries, pensions and perks for Senators and Congressmen are out of control. The lawyer-come-to-Congress knows a deep pockets client when he sees one, and they regularly vote themselves handsome pay increases (to keep up with inflation, you know). The average lifetime pension for Members of Congress is now more than $1.5 million. The tendency of incumbents to stay in office until they die is also well-known. Corruption is endemic to the system. Who can forget the hilarious Abscam operation in which a distinguished Member of Congress grabbed a briefcase full of cash from fake FBI "Arab sheiks" who looked like the villains on Saturday afternoon wrestling?

By now the American people are practically numb to political corruption. They have come to expect it, depriving the lawyer-dominated Congress of the credibility it craves A notorious example of Congressional corruption is the billion dollar savings and loan debacle. The taxpayer got stuck big on that one. The final tab is over $300 billion to cover all the embezzlement and fraud. Payout is to be extended over a decade. Leading the league in savings and loan defaults is Bill Clinton's own state of Arkansas. The so-called Whitewater scandal involves Arkansas savings and loan associations and much more. President and Mrs. Clinton are both attorneys.

The franking privilege (taxpayer financed postage) is widely used to keep incumbent Senators and Congressmen in office. Ever-rising campaign costs—over $550,000 just to run for the House—are another sad fact of political life. Only big money can finance that. Members of Congress are mere tools of political action committees which deal in dollar amounts that average citizens cannot possibly match.

And lest we forget, it is Congress in its supreme arrogance that levies onerous, confiscatory, misery-inducing taxes on Middle America to finance every elite-inspired pork barrel project imaginable. America has the finest Congress that money can buy, and any residue of majority rule has been washed away in a flood of big special interest PAC money.

Representative Government is not at all present in the outrageously unrepresentative makeup of Congress. Ninety percent of working Americans are employees—either white collar salaried workers or blue collar wage workers—but they are virtually absent from both houses of Congress. Following up on the 224 lawyers in the Congress are 187 businessmen and bankers; 163 in the House, and 24 in the Senate. These are rarely small entrepreneurs. Most of them are independently wealthy.

Congress is essentially an assembly of lawyers and their most affluent clients. It functions as little more than a money-laundering institution, expropriating dollars from taxpayers, taking their cut and appropriating the rest to special interests. It is like a giant publicly-funded law firm with the American people as its reluctant client.

Speaking of publicly-funded law firms, the Legal Services Corporation has largely abandoned its charter of helping the poor and evolved into just another bureaucracy of lawyers determined to impose their political agenda on the rest of us.

One creative (to put it politely) idea for reform is "occupational apportionment." This would involve a Constitutional restructuring of Congress by doing away with one of the Houses (probably the Senate, a millionaire's club). This would be replaced with a second House elected on the basis of occupational representation, supplementing the numerically proportional House of Representatives. The argument goes that under occupational apportionment the majority of Americans—working people, retired workers, and unemployed workers—could be represented. The Commerce Department's Dictionary of Occupational Titles could serve as a guide. Would such an innovation give Middle America a shot at some semblance of true representation? As farfetched as it is, could "occupational apportionment" be any worse than the current lawyer/special interest-dominated Congress? Any really bold reform proposals would be deemed "controversial" and "radical" by big media from the start. This is understandable, but the situation is already "radical" and "controversial" by any measure.

There should just be some way to induce Congress to focus on bettering the lot of the average American. Our current government is not representative, though our form of government was designed to be. Representative Government in America has been betrayed—and lawyers have profited immensely from the treachery.

No type of "occupational apportionment" is a possibility, at least for the foreseeable future. Another idea for reform could be to remove political advertising from radio and television, similar to advertising restrictions on cigarettes and hard liquor. Would this curb the vote-buying power of big money? Would it at least discourage debilitating mudslinging campaigns? The authors do not necessarily advocate these measures, but raise them to emphasize that creative thinking is absolutely essential for reform of a thoroughly corrupted, truly broken system.

If Congress were not so dominated by lawyers, would it be less captive to deep pockets special interests? It may well be a conflict of interest to benefit from the practice of law while making that very law. There is no better way to help your livelihood than to make the rules by which you make your money. Should attorneys be barred from holding legislative office?

At least two Congressional reforms are possible, both designed to replace professional politicians with citizen legislators. These reforms are term limits and meaningful campaign finance reform.

The people have spoken on term limits. In 1992 fourteen states voted to impose term limits on their Congressional delegations, including Arkansas. Yet the State Supreme Court of Arkansas struck down the vote of the people calling for terms limits on Members of Congress. When the Arkansas Supreme Court ruling was appealed to the U.S. Supreme Court, President Clinton directed his Solicitor

General to file a brief against the people of Arkansas. Clinton argues that term limits may be imposed on Congress only by constitutional amendment, though he is fully aware that the members of his own party will never support such an amendment.

In May, 1995 the U.S. Supreme Court ruled in a divided five to four decision, that Congressional term limits required a constitutional amendment. They came down squarely on the side of imperial rule from Washington saying that the people didn't vote right, that the people of the individual states are not empowered to set term limits on their own duly elected federal representatives. Once again, the judicial branch, political appointees themselves, defended the professional politicians from the reforms of the people. That ruling, more than most of the elite's dictates, has even further estranged the American people from their already corrupt government. Over time, lessons from that ruling could well serve to expose federal tyranny as much as the government's Waco massacre or ambush of the Randy Weaver family at Ruby Ridge, Idaho.

In their 1994 "Contract With America," Republicans pledged to bring the issue of term limits to a vote in Congress. They never imagined they would be called upon to fulfill their contract. It was a clever publicity stunt, a campaign gimmick for winning GOP Congressional seats in the 1994 election. Most voters interpreted the language of the contract as support for term limits. On the contrary, it was merely support for a vote on the question of term limits. A majority of incumbent GOP House members opposed term limits before the November, 1994 elections. With a great deal of arm twisting, House Speaker Newt Gingrich was able to garner just over 80 percent of GOP House members to support a term limits amendment to the Constitution. Many of them saw it as a safe vote, knowing full well it would fall far short of the two-thirds vote necessary which it did because of overwhelming opposition from Democrat Congressmen.

Although some argue that the GOP takeover of Congress is proof that term limits are not needed, the opposite is true. Fully 91 percent of incumbents running were reelected in the 1994 Congressional elections! Most Republican gains were from races for open seats not held by an incumbent.

The likelihood of Congress even considering meaningful campaign finance reform, such as limits on PAC/special interest contributors and reduced-cost TV and radio time for candidates, is remote at best. Republicans, who have a reputation of antagonism towards working people, need big money to overcome liberal big media in the elite's biennial faction fights (elections). Yet liberal-leaning PACs and special interest groups are also opposed to any public financing of campaigns or other outside-the-status-quo reforms. Former California Governor Jerry Brown ran a strong Democratic Presidential primary campaign with a $100 limit on all contributions. Other ideas are a $100 limit on campaign contributions from anyone, anytime; abolition of the Congressional franking privilege; no radio or television political advertising; and term limits. Another idea would be to allow no contributions originating from outside the state or even Congressional District contested. Some countries do not allow release of polling data for some time prior to elections. Could any or all of these measures serve to clean up the campaign process and bring it closer to the people?

It is in the judicial branch where the reign of lawyers is absolute. The imperial judiciary throws out the vote of the people in a heartbeat when it conflicts with their elitist agenda. This was made perfectly clear with the issue of Congressional term limits.

While the Supreme Court of Arkansas threw out term limits enacted by vote of the people, the Supreme Court of

Illinois blocked term limits from even appearing on the 1994 election ballot. Illinois term limits supporters had filed 437,088 petition signatures calling for a statewide referendum. The proposed "Eight is Enough" term limits measure would limit state legislators to no more than eight years in the Illinois General Assembly. According to a statewide poll published in the *Chicago Tribune*, 70 percent of voters said that they would vote for the term limit amendment if it appeared on the ballot. This was just too much. Soon the Chicago Bar Association (CBA) entered the picture. The CBA, of course, is an organization of lawyers. The CBA had already lobbied the Illinois General Assembly for a judges' pay hike. The CBA filed a lawsuit to block the Eight is Enough referendum from appearing on the ballot. Without explanation the Illinois Supreme Court ruled 4 to 3 in favor of the CBA suit. The CBA did not want their members at the public trough to have a time limit on their feeding. This is a clear example of how the legal industry is at once parasite and predator on the body politic—blocking the peoples right to vote! So much for representative government in America! *What recourse do we have when we don't even have the right to vote?* How can we resist?

Lifetime-appointed Federal Judges are even more arrogant. More than forty years after the Brown vs. Board of Education case, the school systems of Kansas City, Missouri and Little Rock, Arkansas remained under the control of federal judges. These judges have told the homeowners of both Kansas City and Little Rock that if they did not vote for higher property taxes for the schools, then the judges themselves would set the tax rates. When the State of Missouri sought release from federal court for the Kansas City school system, President Clinton ordered the Justice Department to oppose it. Federal judges have ordered both school systems to *establish attitudes in the community and to eliminate group differences in standardized test scores*—goals which have never been attained in other school systems. Stalinist Russia knew how to establish attitudes and eliminate group differences. It is certainly not the American way. It *is* the judges' way—and it is very, very dangerous.

In 1994 the people of California overwhelmingly approved Proposition 187, a simple demand by the people that the state of California enforce existing laws by denying illegal aliens the use of public schools and social services. On December 14, 1994 Federal District Judge Mariana Pfaelzer granted a preliminary injunction blocking almost all of the provisions of Proposition 187. Again, a federal judge had rescued the elite's notion of public policy from any threat posed by a majority vote of the citizens. Again, all Proposition 187 called for was state enforcement of existing laws!

Preeminently arrogant is the U.S. Supreme Court. They are lifetime Presidential appointees and have turned the law—and in the process American society—on its head. Nowhere in the Constitution, or in English common law before it, is supreme power vested in the judiciary. But so it is in our nonrepresentative, lawyer-dominated government. This insanity has gone so far that we no longer have the rule of law, but rule of the judge. Federal courts have gone far beyond their illegitimate role as instruments of social policy; nowadays, judicial opinions are laws; the Federal courts now create law (a function of Congress, if the Constitution mattered). Professors William J. Quirk and R. Randall Bridwell offer a brilliant and compelling study of this problem in their new book, *Judicial Dictatorship*.

In the last forty years, the Supreme Court has achieved what Jefferson warned against: "[The] judiciary of the United States is the subtle corps of sappers and miners constantly working under ground to undermine the foundations of our confederated fabric. They are construing our

Constitution from a co-ordination of a general and special government to a general and supreme one alone."

The Supreme Court is a legislative force stronger than Congress, beyond election or recall by the voters. It does what its members believe that legislators should have done, setting aside whole bodies of statute law and creating new law to carry out its edicts. This has been the effect of the court's forays into the areas of capital punishment, reapportionment, rights of accused criminals, pornography, forced school busing, prayer in schools, and libel and slander laws.

In all of these areas, the Court always rules in favor of the interests of either the elite or the underclass. The Middle American taxpayer has been systematically excluded. The Court itself is virtually a mirror image of the ruling elite. When the elite wishes to signal a change in societal direction, it is often to the Court that it turns.

Legal scholar Professor Lino Graglia has done a great deal of research on politicization of the judiciary: "If politicians are frequently tempted to venality, the professional temptation of judges—overestimation of one's competence—is even more dangerous . . . [Judges] are in fact among the least trustworthy of government officials. This is to be expected, since they are least subject to external restraints." Judges, especially Federal judges, are politicians pure and simple. The very job is a plum political appointment. These aren't doled out because of any professional ability—politics is what matters. And there is nothing like playing politics from the bench, hiding behind the robe and calling it a system of "justice" or "rule of law."

For true government by the people to be restored, the day must come when citizens will demand that judges be treated like the legislators they ape, the politicians they are. This would mean that judges at all levels would be subject to election, recall and term limits.

The domain of regulatory law falls under the executive

branch and is the ideal place where lawyers who may have failed to become federal judges can console themselves playing tyrant. The vast array of outrages committed in the name of regulatory law has been most ably documented by James Bovard in his book, *Lost Rights*.

The mass of regulatory law is accumulated in the *Code of Federal Regulations*. Most often, regulatory law is an immediate problem for employers rather than for Middle American workers. The average employee is already wholly regulated on the job by his supervisor, and even off the job in community life, especially if he is a corporate employee. Needless to say, this inhibits freedom of expression and other avenues of personal development. Many of the regulations seeking to curb corporate abuse against the environment and employee health may have some basis in common sense, but they are enforced by government lawyers in ways detrimental mostly to small business. Multinational corporate attorneys and regulatory law parasites often work well together. The government regulatory lawyer may want a posh corporate job one day.

Regulatory law is most detrimental to Middle Americans through so-called Affirmative Action, which has inevitably become institutionalized discrimination against whites— more specifically against white males. Oversight of a vast array of Affirmative Action programs is handled by the misnamed Equal Employment Opportunity Commission.

Affirmative Action apologists say that it is designed to help minorities, but women are hardly a minority, owning slightly more than half of the assets in America. Affirmative Action is a way to divide Middle America by gender in the already desperate competition for jobs and personal advancement. Those few women who may have benefited from Affirmative Action, mostly of the Hillary Rodham and Janet Reno ilk, are far outweighed by the millions of working women who find that the significant men in their lives can no longer earn enough to provide for them and their families. Not just the traditional male role but also the natural (sociobiological) male role has been destroyed. If someone in the elite maliciously designed a government program to stir contention in the ranks of working Americans, he could not have done better than to have concocted the present Affirmative Action program. This is a boiling cauldron that will not simmer down any time soon.

Judicial dictates, overregulation, Congress and Affirmative Action have a common denominator in lawyers, the merciless shock troops of Middle America's dispossession. The legal system exists to serve the legal industry. It is woefully estranged from the American people it once served. Our current legal system is a far cry from the old English Common Law upon which it was originally based. Even the jury system is collapsing in the face of racial antagonism urged on by those artful manipulators, the lawyers. The legal industry has killed Representative Government in our country. We are now governed in an extra-constitutional mode. A military coup would have accomplished the same, but the legal industry pulled it off without the publicity.

Those who benefit from the current status quo will be the last to act for changing it.

Chapter Ten

What Now?

It is time for the Middle American majority to rouse itself and act. The late 1990s present the best opportunity to take back our country since the Great Betrayal began. Before we act, we must organize. Lack of organization is the most severe impediment. Before we organize, we must fully understand the historical causes of our dispossession and never forget them.

The calamitous Great Depression ravaged the entire industrialized world, toppling an unpopular order and giving rise to big government on both sides of the Atlantic. Then came World War II, leaving the United States and the Soviet Union dominant in the world. The Depression brought about the welfare state; the war gave rise to the military industrial complex. Both were born of massive federal spending. The U.S. response to domestic and global crisis had brought about a statist new order in our country.

While many of the 1930s government programs were helpful in that terrible period, only the war effort ended the Depression. With the war and Depression behind us, a reduction of the military-industrial complex and the welfare state was in order. The emergency was over. But the new status quo, empowered through massive federal spending, was highly profitable for some. Big corporations and banks were necessary to service and finance it, and government itself had become a major societal power base of jobs and other political vote-buying mechanisms. The military-industrial complex and the welfare state were both products of big government and big business (including banks). They joined forces. The corporate welfare state was in place.

Soon foreign aid, beginning with the Marshall Plan, helped the banks and corporations go international. Government programs to help people in the U.S. expanded way beyond their need; but who could argue? America was prosperous. President Lyndon Johnson epitomized the marriage of the welfare state and the military-industrial complex, launching the Great Society and a massive military buildup in Vietnam—both miserable failures.

Over time the military-industrial interests came to dominate the Republican party, and the welfare statists, the Democrats. They needed each other for the spending to continue—they were in it together. If there is any doubt about this, an examination of corporate and banking political contributions is most revealing. Always follow the money for the real story.

The left-right/liberal-conservative divisions were not sufficient to inhibit development of popular middle class movements. Containment and control of popular political expression became a major concern of the elite.

With the Goldwater nomination in 1964, a "movement conservatism" arose within the Republican party. These were anti-welfare-state conservatives. Supported by the military-industrial wing of the elite, they said little about big government's largesse to that sector, instead concentrating their criticism on tax and spend liberals and welfare cheats. With every successive Republican administration, government continued to grow, and taxes increased. The movement conservatives never had a clue. This "right wing" became another weapon of the establishment. In fact every time a real challenge was posed to the status quo, whether George Wallace, John Anderson, or Ross Perot, the loudest denunciations of each came from the conservative movement.

On the "left" side, the old "New Left" came of age in the 1960s. The New Left was an anti-military-industrial complex movement, rallying around opposition to the Vietnam War. Culturally, it was a Marxist movement, vehemently anti-middle class. It initially had very little grassroots support and was largely a creature of academia. Yet, by effectively seizing upon opposition to the Vietnam War, the New Left became a popular movement in American politics. With the full cooperation of big media, the New Left pulled off a major power play spurring the creation of numerous federal programs furthering their agenda. In doing so they succeeded in making over major institutions of American society in their own leftist image. The ceaseless assault of mean-spirited multiculturalism assured the New Left's place in history as the implacable foe of Middle America.

With the politically powerful movement conservatives and culturally dominant New Left, each wing of the elite had its own pet activists. They have been skillfully played off against one another for years in political theater without parallel in modern times. The attention of Middle America is often riveted on these shenanigans. While immigrants pour in, jobs flow out, living standards decline, and crime runs amok, we have been entertained with the Watergate hearings, Iran-Contra, Whitewater, sexual harassment, O.J. Simpson, and lest we forget, those biennial slugfests known as elections. This is high political theatre, playing to a packed house night after night on big media. And it has brought about no substantive change in spite of increasing partisan bitterness.

What better way to control the agenda than to divide American politics between conservative and liberal, right and left? You were either a "red baiter" or "soft on Communism." If you cared about the environment or social security, you had to be on the left (liberal Democratic). If you cared about taxes or national security, the right (conservative Republican) was the pigeonhole for you. If you were against both the Vietnam War and the welfare state, there was no political berth to be found. Meanwhile, the corporate welfare state continued to grow while left and right battled it out about which half of the problem to address.

The division of politics into right and left is a practice more than two hundred years old, and the first order of business should be to get over it. Middle America is mistaken to assume that political left and political right are "sides," one of which must be right and the other wrong. Middle America is the radical center.

The shell game of "right" and "left" has given us a political system offering two extremes. Today's "left" is the driving engine of the welfare state, consisting of liberals dominating the Democrat Party. As the welfare state became more extreme, it grew more oppressive; and initiatives of the left/liberal/Democrat side of the political spectrum are nowadays, to one degree or another, rooted in Marxist ideology.

The right/conservative/Republican side of the spectrum has fallen completely captive to corporate interests, and most of its initiatives are to one degree or another rooted in Libertarian ideology.

This spurious left versus right paradigm has come to be a "Communism versus Capitalism" type of scenario played out within our own system. Liberalism and Conservatism in today's America are all too often simply diluted versions of Marxism or Libertarianism which are two horns of the same bull. Both posit a primitive concept of human nature, that of a purely economic man, devoid of any spiritual, cultural or national dimension. Religious faith, race, culture, nation and quality of life are ignored by both the liberal and conservative branches of today's elite. They see the United States of America as a gigantic piece of real estate where you can make big bucks—nothing less, nothing more. Is it any wonder that working Americans are so abused? They are economic units, pocket change of the elite. Lest we forget: Government and capital exist to serve the people. Our shameless "leaders" today are bought and paid for to believe just the opposite.

Big media dismisses Middle America's deep-seated frustration with the term "angry white males." It is not working. They can no longer pigeonhole our people this way.

In sum, our post-World War II political system has evolved into a giant greed-driven special interest apparatus, headed in the same direction regardless of which party may be in "power." The various left versus right political charades have been quite successful. It is a battle of the elite and its underclass shock troops versus Middle America—not between right and left! This strategy is nothing new. The Romans called it *divide et impera*—divide and conquer. And isn't it amazing how Middle Americans—people with similar values, goals, traditions, and frustrations—have been divided down the middle. So many of the sham political confrontations we have suffered—blue collar versus white collar, Democrat versus Republican—are really American versus American. Special interest bipartisanship has waged war against Middle America and so pervasively corrupted our system of government that the Constitution is treated as little more than an extraneous historical curiosity.

That is a brief history of our problem which explains why the various conservative and liberal initiatives of five decades have seldom yielded a positive result.

Now the Cold War is over, the government is broke, the elite is worried and the demise of Representative Government and dispossession of Middle America are a fact of life. As before in history, enlightened government is often preceded by tyranny. Perhaps this is the utter darkness before the new dawn.

———————

Middle America must unite. Giving political loyalty exclusively to either the Democratic or Republican politicians will not do. Just look at what bipartisanship has done to us with its taxes, deficits, NAFTA, foreign aid and lawyers. Every election we are assured of representation—and that is the end of it. So often the only real partisan competition is between an old national faction of the elite and a newer, more cosmopolitan one.

The U.S. Constitution says nothing about a two-party system, yet it has been effectively legislated into existence. Restrictive campaign finance and ballot access laws written by the two major parties make sure of it. Usually, any third party or political movement is centered around an activist or charismatic personality, like George Wallace, John Anderson or Ross Perot. But third party Presidential campaigns have always failed, and usually bring down the third party with them.

An effective Middle American political movement must be built from the grassroots—beginning with community, local and state organization. This must include an accompanying voice in the popular media, essential to remind us that government and capital should serve the people, not master them. As long as the American people are conditioned to spend, to consume, and to validate very facet of their existence through the money chase and the economic unit world view, greed and other meaningless considerations will divide us.

Middle American activists are building a movement to restore Representative Government in America. This popular effort already includes a national newspaper, *Middle American News*. Talk radio is now a mechanism of Middle

American empowerment just like concealed carry laws, defended markets and lower taxes. Make no mistake about it—media presence is very important.

Big media will either ignore this people's movement or be bitterly hostile to it. This is to be expected and is not of immediate concern. Our concern without distraction should be the awakening of Middle America. That is of paramount importance. The discredited big media's seal of approval is of no concern. Remember this every time the evening news tells us who is in or out and what is good or bad.

The existing political structure, craving credibility, can occasionally be utilized to our advantage. Activation of sympathetic factions within the parties and their alliance with nonpartisan independents should not be discouraged. This would be as much an exercise in education as political activism. Such collaboration should be undertaken only when it serves to raise the consciousness of Middle America as a single people. The prospect of petty electoral success should not blind us from this goal. A knavish politician sells his soul for big media approval faster than a cur begs scraps—this should no longer be our problem.

If a political label is to be placed on the knowledge that government and capital exist to serve the people, it cannot be conservative, liberal or moderate. It is simply Middle America, the vital center—the bedrock of American democratic representative government and the American nation. Middle America will transcend false barriers of occupational affiliation, social standing, partisanship and geography.

The political rise of the vital center will occur outside of the two-party system, but will no doubt have considerable interaction with it. For an indefinite period, the movement will build as an invisible party above parties, essential to the electoral success of either party but beholden to neither. Only from a leverage point of strength outside the bipartisan system can Middle America grow in political power enough to effectively oppose the corrupt status quo.

What must be understood is that Middle American mobilization is more than running for office, publishing a newspaper or making the air waves. It is strengthening the family, restoring the neighborhood and rebuilding the community. This all begins at home and requires no validation whatsoever from any mouthpiece of the establishment. We are at the point that whatever big media attempts to thrust upon us should be rejected out of hand. One thing is certain: it is incumbent upon us all—individuals, families, communities—to lead without greed. Lead through example; simply throw off the shackles and lead.

Americans by the hundreds of thousands must resolve to do this. Leadership begins at home. The fruits of our labor will take hold if each of us will set aside some little time each month to do something—talk to neighbors, fellow employees, retirees and students, write letters to newspapers, call talk radio programs, distribute extra copies of *Middle American News* and work the computer bulletin boards. Becoming active in the nonpolitical organizations is also important. This is a struggle for the soul of our country which does not end at the factory gate. Hold your own meetings and invite candidates and the public. This is just one more activity essential to reclaiming our lost citizenship. It requires no money—just patriotic involvement.

Our efforts must be dedicated to the restoration of Representative Government through Middle American empowerment. We must be free of the ideological rigidity afflicting many well-meaning conservative, liberal, public interest and patriotic organizations. Such groups often promote well-intentioned programs to defend against crime, consumer fraud, confiscatory taxes and worker deprivation, all the while accepting much of the selfish, nation-wrecking policies of the corporate welfare state.

Well-intentioned organizations labor for the public good on all manner of issues. While helpful, the narrow scope of single issue advocacy cannot address the broadly based concerns of Middle America. Well-meaning idealists will journey to the belly of the beast and finance professional Washington representation. Lobbyists are invariably co-opted by their environment, claiming advancement of their cause through big media access or other crumbs from the establishment table. Genuine progress comes from the hinterlands. Turning from Washington, New York and Hollywood and setting our sights on America's greatest resource—our people, a single people—holds the key to success. We must organize, organize even more, organize yet again, as churches organize the faithful. The mobilization of Middle America is a higher calling, certain to restore the legacy left us by the Founding Fathers, the very model of an elite.

The American people are in a race against time. The greedy international-minded elite has consolidated its hold on the ship of state. This is a challenge the likes of which has never been faced before in our history. Our situation is similar to that of an army whose officer corps has deserted. Abandoned in the field, we still have the resources to prevail, but only if we are resourceful and resolved. In such a state we can discern any number of sinister forces which have contributed to the problem. Yet blaming outside forces for our own weakness definitively confirms it. Our difficulties, onerous as they may seem, are merely symptoms of the deeper moral and spiritual crisis gripping our entire civilization. Our lack of resolve, which is ultimately responsible for our dispossession, is our problem, and ours alone. Courage cannot be instilled in an ailing body politic like medicine given a sick patient. We must heal ourselves and reclaim resolve. We will then prevail. Many times supreme effort is demanded for the most simple of endeavors. Thus is the mission to take back our country.

Middle Americans can do this by looking to themselves and assuming absolute responsibility for every facet of their lives. This may prove difficult at first, as decades of conditioning must be unlearned, false premises discarded, selfishness expunged and respect reclaimed. To do this we must avoid the dead-ends of outmoded ideology, acquire an historical perspective and avoid the mistakes of past organizations.

In the darkest days of the life of our nation, when the dispossessed working American labors helplessly amid the ashes of Representative Government, a force is appearing which will not leave the fate of future generations to our betrayers. Raised from neighborhoods with the memory of a better life, building community in the face of globe-encircling greed, roused from the slumber of indifference and indoctrination, and sustained by the spirit of the Founding Fathers, Middle America is on the march. Mobilized anew and wise in the ways of citizen action, America is aroused. The Great Betrayal can be undone, and a greater nation will be forged by a determined people.

It will not be an easy course. As fifty-six of our early leaders knew, the path of least resistance is not an option. Disfavor and disappointment will be no strangers along the way. Neither will the resolve which bonds us. Stand up and be counted. Speak out. Lead through your example. Be of good courage, ever vigilant and faithful through and through. With Truth on our side, victory is ours if only we will seize it. Join us in this noble cause.

About the Authors

LOUIS T. MARCH, a North Carolina native, acquired firsthand knowledge of the big business/big government axis as a U.S. Senate aide and Washington lobbyist. He is an independent businessman with a strong interest in historic preservation, and serves as Chairman of the Representative Government Education Foundation.

BRENT NELSON, who is a native of Ohio, attended Capital University, Ohio University and the University of Kentucky. A Ph.D. in English language and literature, he has taught at several colleges in the Midwest. Nelson is also the author of *America Balkanized: Immigration's Challenge to Government.*

The authors invite comments and suggestions from you, the reader, and may be written to in care of:

Representative Government Press
P. O. Box 97668
Raleigh, North Carolina 27624

ORDER FORM

FOR ADDITIONAL COPIES OF
The Great Betrayal

Name _____

Address _____

_____

City_____ State _____ Zip_____

(All prices include postage and handling)

☐ 1 copy $5.95
☐ 2-24 copies $3.00 each
☐ 25 or more copies $2.00 each

Total number of copies ordered _____ = $ _____
(Please make checks payable to:
Representative Government Press or RGP)

Mail this form (or a copy) to:
Representative Government Press
P. O. Box 97668
Raleigh, NC 27624

We will be happy to send *The Great Betrayal* directly to your friends. Please enclose the name and address of the person to receive the book as well as payment of $5.95 for each name listed.

ORDER FORM

FOR ADDITIONAL COPIES OF
The Great Betrayal

Name _____

Address _____

_____

City_____ State _____ Zip_____

(All prices include postage and handling)

☐ 1 copy $5.95
☐ 2-24 copies $3.00 each
☐ 25 or more copies $2.00 each

Total number of copies ordered _____ = $ _____
(Please make checks payable to:
Representative Government Press or RGP)

Mail this form (or a copy) to:
Representative Government Press
P. O. Box 97668
Raleigh, NC 27624

We will be happy to send *The Great Betrayal* directly to your friends. Please enclose the name and address of the person to receive the book as well as payment of $5.95 for each name listed.